Credit Card Hacks: Tips on Maximizing Rewards and Benefits

Genalin Jimenez

TABLE OF CONTENTS

Chapter 1. Introduction to Credit Card Rewards
Overview of credit card rewards programs.
Understanding the different types of rewards (cashback, points, miles).

Chapter 2. Choosing the Right Card for Your Lifestyle
How to assess spending habits?
Matching your lifestyle with the best rewards card.

Chapter 3. Sign-Up Bonuses and How to Leverage Them
Tips for maximizing sign-up bonuses.
Understanding spending requirements and timelines.

Chapter 4. Maximizing Cashback Opportunities
Tips for earning cashback on everyday purchases.
Leveraging rotating categories for bonus cashback.

Chapter 5. Using Points and Miles Wisely
How to earn and redeem points and miles effectively.
Strategies for stretching the value of points and miles.

Chapter 6. Understanding Transfer Partners
Benefits of transferring points to airline and hotel partners.
Maximizing value through strategic point transfers.

Chapter 7. Utilizing Introductory 0% APR Offers
How to use 0% APR offers for big purchases or balance transfers.
Avoiding pitfalls when the introductory period ends.

Chapter 8. Combining Multiple Cards for Optimal Rewards

Tips for using multiple cards to maximize benefits.
Creating a strategy for category and general spending.

Chapter 9. Exploiting Quarterly and Annual Category Bonuses
Tracking and utilizing bonus categories.
Setting reminders to activate rotating categories.

Chapter 10. Travel Perks and Benefits
Understanding common travel perks (e.g., no foreign transaction fees, travel insurance).
Maximizing lounge access, baggage benefits, and upgrades.

Chapter 11. Dining and Grocery Rewards
Identifying cards with strong dining and grocery rewards.
How to earn cashback or points on essential spending?

Chapter 12. Maximizing Online Shopping Rewards
Using credit card shopping portals and cashback sites.
Stack rewards through online shopping offers and partnerships.

Chapter 13. Taking Advantage of Referral Bonuses
Earning extra points by referring friends and family.
Understanding referral limits and bonus structures.

Chapter 14. Credit Card Reward Multipliers and Special Deals
Finding cards with higher multipliers for frequent purchases.
Tips for seasonal and promotional rewards multipliers.

Chapter 15. Understanding Annual Fees and Justifying Their Cost
How to evaluate if an annual fee is worth it.
Using perks and rewards to offset the fee.

Chapter 16. Avoiding Common Pitfalls to Maximize Rewards

Tips for avoiding interest and fees that can negate rewards.
How to manage payments to avoid penalties?

Chapter 17. Building and Protecting Your Credit Score

Understanding how responsible credit card use builds credit.
Tips for protecting your score while maximizing rewards.

Chapter 18. Advanced Redemption Techniques

Tips for redeeming points for the highest value (e.g., first-class travel, luxury hotels).
How to avoid low-value redemptions.

Chapter 19. Leveraging Cardholder Benefits Beyond Rewards

Benefits like purchase protection, extended warranties, and price matching.
Making the most of rental car insurance, travel insurance, and concierge services.

Chapter 20. Final Tips on Staying Organized and Tracking Rewards

Best practices for tracking rewards and expiration dates.
Tools and apps for managing multiple cards and reward points.

ABOUT THE AUTHOR

The author is a trying hard writer who believes there is no harm in trying, there is gain in hoping, and there is magic in believing!

Credit Card Hacks: Tips on Maximizing Rewards and Benefits

Chapter 1
Introduction to Credit Card Rewards

In the contemporary landscape of personal finance, credit cards serve not only as tools for convenience but also as vehicles for financial reward. With the surge of various credit card rewards programs, consumers are presented with a myriad of choices designed to enhance the card-use experience. This chapter will delve into the essence of credit card rewards programs, offering an overview of their structure, the motivations behind their development, and an explanation of the different types of rewards available to cardholders.

Overview of Credit Card Rewards Programs: Credit card rewards programs are incentive structures offered by credit card issuers to encourage spending and loyalty among consumers. By utilizing these programs, cardholders can earn rewards for everyday purchases, making their credit card transactions more fruitful. Whether one is buying groceries, booking travel, or simply filling their tank with gas, each swipe of a card can contribute to a future reward.

The primary appeal of these rewards programs lies in their ability to enhance the value derived from using a credit card. In essence, consumers are rewarded for their spending behavior, a unique concept that transitions the act of purchasing from just a transactional process to a value-generating endeavor. Furthermore, the competitive landscape among credit card issuers has given rise to a plethora of options, ensuring there is likely a program suitable for every consumer's spending habits.

Credit card rewards can take various forms, each designed to meet different consumer needs. For instance, some individuals may prioritize cashback for its simplicity and straightforward value, while others might find greater benefit in points or miles that can be redeemed for travel services or experiences. Additionally, many programs are tiered, where cardholders can ascend through levels of rewards based on their spending, unlocking greater benefits and more exclusive options as they progress.

Understanding the Different Types of Rewards: When considering credit card rewards, understanding the various types currently available is essential for making an informed decision about which card best suits one's financial lifestyle. Here, we will categorize and explain the three predominant types of rewards: cashback, points, and miles, as well as the advantages and limitations associated with each.

Cashback Rewards: Cashback rewards are perhaps the most straightforward and attractive type of reward for many consumers. As their name suggests, they offer a percentage of the amount spent back to the cardholder in the form of cash. This can typically range from 1% to as much as 5% or more depending on the type of purchase and the terms of the card. For instance, a cardholder could earn 5% cashback on groceries, 2% on dining, and 1% on all other purchases.

The primary advantage of cashback rewards is their simplicity. Cardholders can easily see the value of their rewards as actual money returned to them, making it easier to conceptualize the benefits of using the card. Additionally, cashback rewards can be redeemed in various ways, such as statement credits, direct deposits, or gift cards, providing flexibility in how the rewards are utilized.

However, cashback cards can also have drawbacks. Often, the higher cashback rates apply only to select categories or have maximum earning limits, which may not entirely capture a consumer's typical spending patterns. Furthermore, some promotional offers may only be available for the first year or under specific conditions, potentially leading to consumer disappointment when those enticing rates expire.

Points Rewards: Points rewards programs operate on a different system, whereby customers earn points for every dollar spent. While the earning rate differs from card to card, it's not uncommon for consumers to earn 1 point per dollar, with many cards offering bonus points for purchases in specific categories, like travel or dining.

These points can typically be redeemed for various rewards, including merchandise, gift cards, statement credits, and travel discounts. Some credit cards collaborate with specific retailers or travel partners, which can yield additional value for points earned. This flexibility allows savvy cardholders to maximize the worth of the rewards based on their interests and preferences.

One potential pitfall of points rewards, however, is the complexity of understanding their value. Points can often have fluctuating redemption rates and may expire if not used within a designated timeframe. Additionally, the fine print associated with point systems can be complicated, leading to confusion over how rewards are accumulated and redeemed. For consumers who do not often travel or shop at partnered retailers, the value derived from points rewards may not argue as compellingly as cashback offers.

Miles Rewards: Miles rewards are specifically tailored for travel enthusiasts and typically cater to those who consistently fly with certain airlines or prefer to book lodgings through associated hotel chains. When spending money, cardholders accrue miles, with one mile often equivalent to one dollar spent on the airline or travel partner. Many airlines and hotel chains offer dedicated credit cards that focus on miles' accumulation, providing additional benefits such as free checked bags, priority boarding, and access to exclusive lounges.

The appeal of miles' rewards lies prominently in travel-related perks, including the possibility of free or discounted flights, hotel stays, and unique travel experiences. Cardholders often find that their miles can offer significant value, particularly during promotions or when redeeming for long-haul flights that can be quite pricey when booked with cash.

However, as with the points system, miles can introduce complexities. The redemption process can be fraught with restrictions, such as blackout dates and limited seat availability. Additionally, frequent flyer miles can expire relatively quickly if certain spending thresholds or travel requirements are not met, which can lead many consumers to feel less secure in the value of their earned rewards.

Understanding credit card rewards programs and the various types available, cashback, points, and miles, is essential for consumers looking to derive maximum benefit from their spending. Each type of reward serves different needs, and the value one perceives will ultimately be shaped by individual priorities and lifestyle choices. As credit card issuers continue to innovate and compete, staying informed about these evolving rewards structures will empower consumers to make wise financial decisions and turn everyday spending into real-world benefits.

In the forthcoming chapters, we will elaborate on strategies for selecting the best rewards card for your lifestyle, as well as tips for optimizing rewards accumulation, ensuring that you can unlock the full potential of your credit card rewards experience.

$$$$$$$$$

Chapter 2

Choosing the Right Card for Your Lifestyle

Selecting the right credit card can be a daunting task, especially with the multitude of options available in the market today. The appropriate rewards card can significantly amplify your financial benefits and enhance everyday spending experiences. However, the key to reaping those rewards lies in aligning your credit card choice with your unique spending habits and lifestyle needs. This chapter will guide you through assessing your spending habits and matching those patterns with the most suitable rewards card options.

How to Assess Spending Habits? Before diving into the various types of rewards cards, it's crucial to take a step back and evaluate your financial behavior. Understanding how and where you spend money will help you identify which card features and rewards will benefit you the most. Here are some practical steps to assess your spending habits effectively:

1. Track Your Monthly Expenses: Begin by tracking your monthly expenses over a few months to create a detailed overview of your financial activity. This can be done using various methods, such as:

Budgeting Apps: Utilize digital budgeting tools that categorize spending automatically and provide insights into where your money goes each month.

Spreadsheets: Create a simple spreadsheet to manually log and categorize your expenses. This method allows for customization and deeper personal insight.

Bank Statements: Review your bank statements carefully to identify recurring payments, as well as the categories where you spend the most.

2. Categorize Your Spending: Once you have a record of your monthly expenses, categorize them into groups such as:

Groceries: Include food purchases, household items, and any food delivery services.

Dining Out: Track restaurants, cafes, and takeout spending.

Travel: Include airfare, accommodation, and related expenses such as gas if you drive for trips.

Entertainment: Capture spending on movies, concerts, subscriptions (like Netflix and Spotify), and recreational activities.

Utilities and Bills: Account for monthly payments like electricity, water, internet, and phone bills.

Miscellaneous: Any irregular or unexpected expenses that don't fall into the previous categories.

Understanding these categories will provide valuable insights into your financial behaviors and priorities.

3. Analyze Your Spend Frequency and Preferences: Assess not just how much you spend in each category but also how frequently you incur those expenses. Consider questions such as:

Which categories do I spend the most on per month?

Am I a frequent traveler, or do I usually dine out?

Do I prioritize online shopping, or do I prefer in-store purchases?

Am I likely to pay off my balance each month or carry high balances?

This analysis will help clarify which rewards are most likely to be beneficial to you. For instance, if you find that you frequently dine out but rarely travel, a rewards card that offers higher points or cashback for dining would better serve your spending patterns.

4. Set Financial Goals: In addition to understanding your current spending habits, consider what your financial goals are. Do you wish to maximize travel rewards? Are you looking to save on everyday purchases? Your goals can influence your credit card choice. For example:

If travel is on your horizon, you might aim for a card that offers bonus miles or travel perks.

If you're focused on building an emergency fund, a cashback card that rewards low-risk expenses may be more suitable.

By clarifying your goals, you can select a card that aligns with your aspirations.

Matching Your Lifestyle with the Best Rewards Card: After conducting a thorough assessment of your spending habits, it's time to align those habits with the credit card options available on the market. Here are some key factors to consider when matching your lifestyle with the best rewards card:

1. Types of Rewards Programs: Based on your spending analysis, determine which type of rewards program appeals to you the most, cashback, points, or miles. Each has various strengths depending on your spending patterns:

Cashback: Ideal for those who prefer simplicity and immediate gratification. If your spending is spread across multiple categories rather than focused within a few, then a flat-rate cashback card may work best. Additionally, if your usage frequently involves everyday purchases, groceries, gas, and bills, seeking a card that offers enhanced cashback rates in those categories could be highly beneficial.

Points: If you enjoy the flexibility of redeeming for a wide range of rewards, including merchandise and travel rewards, consider cards that offer points. A rewards card with bonus points in categories important to you (e.g., groceries or dining) could maximize your earned value.

Miles: If travel is central to your lifestyle, whether for business or leisure, consider a card specifically tied to airlines or hotel chains. These often provide exceptional benefits like free checked bags and access to exclusive travel services, generating long-term value for frequent travelers.

2. Evaluate Cardholder Perks and Benefits: Look for additional perks associated with rewards cards, as these can enhance the overall value. Some common benefits include:

Sign-up Bonuses: Many cards offer generous sign-up bonuses for meeting a minimum spending requirement within a specified timeframe. This can provide an excellent boost to your rewards accumulation.

Introductory APR Offers: Some cards come with 0% APR on purchases or balance transfers for an introductory period. If you're planning a significant purchase or need to transfer a high-interest balance, this feature may be advantageous in managing your finances without accruing interest.

No Foreign Transaction Fees: If you travel internationally often, selecting a card that waives foreign transaction fees can lead to significant savings while abroad.

Purchase Protection and Extended Warranty: Cards that provide additional coverage on purchases can offer peace of mind when spending on larger items.

3. Card Fees and Interest Rates: While rewards are appealing, it's also essential to consider any associated fees and interest rates. Look for the following:

Annual Fees: Some premium cards with extensive benefits charge annual fees. Evaluate whether the perks outweigh the costs based on your spending habits. If the rewards you earn exceed the annual fee, the card may be worthwhile.

Interest Rates: If you occasionally carry a balance, consider cards with lower interest rates. While rewards are excellent, high-interest charges can quickly offset any benefits.

Foreign Transaction Fees: As mentioned earlier, if you frequently travel, select a card that doesn't charge foreign transaction fees, which can accumulate significantly during international trips.

4. Flexibility in Redemption: Finally, consider how easy it is to redeem your rewards. A card should offer flexibility that aligns with your preferences. For example:

If you prefer instant gratification, cashback rewards may be your best option.

If you want to accumulate points for larger purchases or experiences, a program with extensive redemption options may be more beneficial.

If you tend to travel often, evaluate the redemption policies for flights and hotels associated with mileage rewards, including any restrictions or blackout dates.

Choosing the right credit card can greatly enhance your financial journey when it aligns with your spending habits and lifestyle. By conducting an honest assessment of your expenses, categorizing your spending, and setting clear financial goals, you can identify the rewards structure that suits you best.

Whether your objective is to receive cashback on everyday purchases, accumulate points for travel, or maximize airline miles, understanding the nuances of credit card rewards programs will enable you to make informed decisions. In upcoming chapters, we will explore how to optimize rewards accumulation and redemption strategies further, ensuring that your credit card experience is as rewarding as possible. Ultimately, the right card can transform your everyday spending into extraordinary benefits, enriching your financial life and enhancing your experiences.

$$$$$$$$

Chapter 3

Sign-Up Bonuses and How to Leverage Them

In the competitive world of credit cards, sign-up bonuses stand out as lucrative incentives that can significantly boost the value of a new cardholder's experience. Offered by many credit card issuers, these bonuses serve as a welcoming gift to new cardholders, often in the form of points, miles, or cashback, upon meeting specific spending thresholds within a designated timeframe. This chapter will explore the dynamics of sign-up bonuses, providing useful tips for maximizing these offers and a clear understanding of the associated requirements and timelines.

Tips for Maximizing Sign-Up Bonuses: If leveraged correctly, sign-up bonuses can add unparalleled value to your financial portfolio! Here are some strategic tips to help you secure these bonuses effectively:

1. Choose the Right Card with a Valuable Sign-Up Offer: Not all sign-up bonuses are created equal; they vary in terms of value and relevance to your lifestyle. Begin by evaluating several factors before selecting your card:

Understanding the Bonus Value: Look beyond the surface. Some cards may advertise a high number of points or miles, but their value can fluctuate based on how you can redeem them. Calculate the actual dollar value of the sign-up bonus to determine if it meets your needs.

Alignment with Spending Patterns: Pick a card whose bonus categories align with your regular spending habits. For example, if you frequently dine out, a card that offers extra bonus points for restaurant purchases will allow you to accumulate the bonus more quickly.

Card Flexibility: Consider cards that allow you to redeem rewards in ways that suit your lifestyle. For instance, a card providing a sign-up bonus that can be redeemed for travel, cashback, or merchandise may offer more versatility.

2. Plan Your Spending to Meet the Requirements: Once you've chosen a card that suits your needs, it's vital to strategize your spending to meet the required minimum during the specified timeframe to secure the sign-up bonus. Here are some effective tactics:

Assess Your Upcoming Purchases: Review your budget and identify essential expenses you already plan to make in the coming months. Major purchases, such as appliances, home improvements, or planned travel, can contribute to meeting the spending requirement without overspending.

Use the Card for Everyday Expenses: Utilize your credit card for routine purchases like groceries, gas, dining, and subscriptions. This practice can help you reach the spending threshold while continuing with your regular budget.

Combine Spending with Family or Friends: If you have a family member or friend with a similar spending appetite or needs, consider combining purchases. You can use your card for shared expenses and reimburse each other. For instance, group costs like gifts or household items can be useful ways to maximize spending with minimal personal impact.

3. Timing Your Application: Timing is critical in the pursuit of sign-up bonuses. Consider the following strategies to optimize your application timing:

Apply When You Have Anticipated Expenses: Assess your calendar for upcoming expenses or planned purchases within the sign-up bonus window. Aligning the card application with significant life events, such as vacations, holiday shopping, or large home projects, can allow you to reach the threshold more effortlessly.

Know Your Financial Patterns: Avoid applying for new cards during financially challenging periods in your personal life (e.g., during an expected job loss or other large expenses) that may impact your ability to utilize your credit line effectively.

Beware of Rapid Applications: While it may be tempting to sign up for multiple cards simultaneously for various bonuses, be cautious. Lenders often scrutinize new accounts opened in quick succession, which could negatively impact your credit score. Stick with one or two applications at a time.

4. Track Your Progress: Once you've secured your new card and begun utilizing it for strategic spending, it's essential to monitor your progress toward meeting the spending requirement:

Use Mobile Banking Tools: Leverage features within your card issuer's mobile app or website to track how much you've spent toward your bonus. This information helps keep you motivated and on target.

Set Personal Reminders: Consider setting reminders to ensure you're hitting certain spending goals throughout the month, enabling you to strategize actions as necessary to meet the requirement.

Understanding Spending Requirements and Timelines: To effectively capitalize on sign-up bonuses, it's vital to have a robust understanding of the spending requirements and timelines specified by the credit card issuer. Here's an overview of key aspects to consider:

1. Minimum Spending Requirements: Credit cards typically set a minimum spending threshold that you must reach within a specific period, often referred to as the "bonus period." This threshold can vary dramatically between cards and may be influenced by factors like the card's annual fee and the attractiveness of the bonus itself. Here are some takeaways regarding minimum spending requirements:

Know What Counts: Review the terms and conditions of the bonus to see what purchases qualify. For example, some cards may exclude certain transactions, like balance transfers or cash advances, from counting towards the threshold. Ensure you are aware of what expenditures qualify so you can plan properly.

Length of the Bonus Period: Most cards specify a time frame, typically 3 months, within which you must meet the spending requirement. However, some premium cards may offer longer periods. Familiarizing yourself with this timeframe is crucial, as you must act quickly to reach your goal while adhering to your normal spending habits.

2. Understanding Timelines and Expiration: Tokens earned via sign-up bonuses can come with certain restrictions or expiration dates. It is important to understand these nuances:

When Does the Timer Start? In most cases, the countdown for the bonus period starts from the date you are approved for the card, not when you activate it. Make sure to factor this in when planning expenditures accordingly.

Expiration of Rewards: After earning your sign-up bonus, check if there's an expiration date on when you must use them. Depending on the card issuer, points, miles, or cashback can have differing expiration policies, and failing to redeem rewards before they expire could negate newfound savings.

Term Definitions: Always read the fine print. It often contains vital information about the bonus conditions, like how long you have to fulfill the spending requirement and any potential fees.

3. Additional Factors to Watch Out for: Beyond the basic requirements, it's also essential to be cognizant of certain factors that may affect your ability to secure or maximize bonuses:

Account Level Restrictions: Some issuers may limit the number of times you can earn a sign-up bonus for the same card. If you have previously held a specific card, also check whether reapplying will allow you to collect the bonus again.

Market Changes: Occasionally, card issuers might change their offers or bonuses. If you wait too long, the offer might vary or no longer be available. Keep an eye on market trends, comparable cards, and any notifications from the issuer regarding potential changes.

Impact on Credit Score: Keep in mind that applying for new credit cards can impact your credit score. Too many inquiries can cause a decline in your score temporarily, and understanding how this can affect loan applications, mortgage rates, and other finance endeavors is critical.

Sign-up bonuses can provide substantial benefits to both new and existing cardholders, enabling you to maximize value with smart planning.

By thoroughly evaluating potential credit cards, strategizing your spending, aligning your application timing with anticipated purchases, and diligently tracking your progress, you can successfully secure these bonuses and enhance your rewards experience.

It's equally essential to have a comprehensive understanding of the spending requirements and the timelines involved. By being aware of what is needed to qualify for these offers, such as the duration of the bonus period, the types of expenditures that count, and how expiration policies work, you will be well-equipped to take full advantage of the rewards program.

As we move to the next chapter, we will delve deeper into strategies for ongoing rewards accumulation beyond sign-up bonuses, ensuring an enduring relationship with your credit card that continues to generate financial benefits over time. With the right knowledge and tactics, you can transform sign-up bonuses into meaningful rewards that align with your financial goals.

$$$$$$$$$

Chapter 4

Maximizing Cashback Opportunities

Cashback credit cards have become a popular choice for consumers looking to stretch their dollars further and earn rewards on everyday purchases. Unlike traditional rewards programs that may offer points or miles, cashback cards provide a straightforward approach, returning a portion of your spending as actual cash.

In this chapter, we will explore various strategies to maximize cashback opportunities, including tips for earning cashback on everyday purchases and leveraging rotating categories for bonus cashback.

Tips for Earning Cashback on Everyday Purchases: Maximizing cashback on everyday purchases is key to elevating your rewards potential. Whether you're buying groceries, fueling your car, or paying for monthly bills, there are several strategies to ensure you earn the maximum cashback possible:

1. Choose the Right Cashback Card: Selecting a credit card tailored to your spending habits is the first step in earning cashback effectively. Here's how to ensure you have the best card for your needs:

Assess Your Spending Habits: Review your monthly expenses to determine where you spend the most. Choose a card that offers higher cashback rates in those categories. For instance, if you frequently dine out, look for a card that offers 3% or more cashback on restaurant purchases.

Consider Flat-Rate Cashback Cards: If your spending varies significantly each month or you don't want to track different categories, a flat-rate cashback card might be ideal. These cards typically offer a consistent percentage (e.g., 1.5% to 2%) on all purchases, making it easy to earn cashback without added complexity.

Check for Sign-Up Bonuses: When selecting a card, look for initial offers that include sign-up bonuses that exceed the cost of the card's annual fee (if applicable). This can help you accumulate additional cashback right away if you are already planning to make significant purchases.

2. Use Cashback Apps and Websites: In addition to using cashback credit cards, you can further maximize your rewards by leveraging cashback apps and websites:

Cashback Apps: Many apps allow users to earn cashback on both in-store and online purchases. Popular options include Rakuten, Ibotta, and Swagbucks. These apps often partner with retailers to provide additional cashback on specific purchases.

Online Shopping Portals: Before making online purchases, visit cashback websites that provide links to major retailers. By clicking through these portals, you can earn a percentage of your purchase price back, sometimes stacking it with your credit card's cashback rewards.

Digital Coupons: Combine cashback offers with digital coupons available through apps or retailer websites. Using a coupon on a purchase can amplify your total savings while also earning cashback.

3. Utilize Online Grocery and Meal Delivery Services: In the era of convenience, online grocery shopping and meal delivery services are booming. Many cashback cards offer enhanced rewards for these expenditures:

Choose Online Grocery Services: Some cashback credit cards offer higher cashback rates on online grocery purchases. If you routinely order groceries online, select a credit card that rewards those transactions accordingly.

Meal Kit and Delivery Bonuses: Explore cashback opportunities for meal kit delivery services (like Blue Apron) or food delivery services (like DoorDash). Some cards promote promotional periods where using their card with these services yields higher cashback.

4. Pay Your Monthly Bills with Cashback Cards: Transform everyday expenses like utility bills, subscriptions, and telecom payments into a cashback opportunity:

Set Up Recurring Payments: Consider switching to a cashback card for recurring bill payments, such as electricity, gas, Netflix, and Amazon Prime. These regular expenses can help you accumulate cashback without needing to adjust your spending habits materially.

Payment Platforms: Platforms like PayPal allow you to pay bills with your credit card, often providing cashback capabilities even if certain bills typically don't accept credit cards. Ensure that there's no additional fee for using your card to avoid jeopardizing your cashback benefits.

5. Be Strategic with All Purchases: Evaluating your purchases and being strategic about when and how you pay can help maximize your cashback returns:

Participate in Promotions: Keep an eye out for promotions or special offers. Card issuers frequently have targeted cashback events, offering increased cashback in specific categories for limited timeframes.

Group Purchases: If you're planning a large purchase, consider combining purchases with family or friends (like gift buying). Use your credit card for the purchase and have them reimburse you, thus reaching higher cashback rewards for larger expenditures.

Year-End Spending: If you're close to another cashback tier or requirement as the year comes to an end, consider making that significant planned expense before the deadline. This strategy can help push you to the next cashback level before the year resets.

Leveraging Rotating Categories for Bonus Cashback: Many cashback credit cards come with the added perk of rotating categories where cardholders can earn elevated cashback rates on select categories for a limited time. Leveraging these rotating categories strategically can significantly enhance your cashback potential.

1. Understanding Rotating Categories: Rotating categories typically change every quarter, allowing you to earn a higher percentage of cashback on specific spending categories such as: Gas Station

Purchases, Dining Out, Groceries, Online Shopping, Travel and Hotels.

For instance, your card may offer 5% cashback on grocery purchases during one quarter and 5% on gas in the next. Recognizing how and when these categories rotate is essential for maximizing your rewards.

2. Stay Informed about Category Changes: To take full advantage of rotating categories, staying informed is critical:

Sign Up for Alerts: Many credit card issuers allow you to sign up for alerts or notifications about upcoming changes to cashback categories. This ensures that you're always aware of when new categories take effect.

Check the Issuer's Website: Regularly visit the credit card issuer's website to check for updates or promotional offers regarding rotating categories. Some issuers even provide suggestions on how to earn more cashback during the promotional periods.

3. Adapt Your Spending Habits Accordingly: Once you know the categories that will provide elevated cashback, adapt your spending habits to align with those opportunities:

Plan Ahead: In the weeks leading up to the start of a new rotation period, strategize your spending. For instance, if you know that groceries will earn 5% cashback, do your grocery shopping at the beginning of the quarter.

Consider Timing for Large Purchases: If you're considering significant purchases that fall within a rotating category, time these expenses strategically around the promotional period start dates.

Utilize Bonus Offers: Occasionally, issuers may provide additional incentives for spending in certain categories during promotional periods. Take full advantage of these special offers to get the most rewards possible.

4. Combining Card Use with Rotating Categories: If you have multiple cashback cards, maximize your rewards by combining their benefits strategically:

Accumulate Maximum Rewards: If one card offers a higher percentage of cashback in a rotating category than another, use that card exclusively for those purchases. For example, if one card offers 5% cashback on dining, and another card offers 3%, prioritize using the higher-percentage card during promotional periods.

Monitor and Adjust Usage: As the promotional periods shift, continue to adjust which card you are using for specific purchases. This flexibility maximizes your overall cashback earnings.

5. Redeem Wisely: Finally, understand the best methods for redeeming cashback from rotating categories:

Know the Redemption Policies: Some cashback cards have different redemption options (e.g., statement credits, direct deposits, or gift cards). Familiarize yourself with how to redeem that cashback effectively.

Watch for Expiration Dates: Ensure you redeem your cashback before it expires. While many cashback programs allow you to accumulate rewards indefinitely, some may have specific terms regarding expiration if your account becomes inactive.

Maximizing cashback opportunities requires a strategic approach that revolves around everyday purchases, smart use of cashback cards, and harnessing rotating categories. By choosing the right credit cards aligned with your spending habits, using cashback apps, strategically planning your purchases, and staying informed about rotating categories, you can optimize your cashback rewards significantly.

Cashback accumulations are not just about the transactions; they are about transforming your everyday expenses into rewards that can enhance your financial situation and lifestyle. As you move forward, implementing these strategies will empower you to make the most of your purchases, turning necessary spending into powerful rewards that add undeniable value to your financial journey.

In the upcoming chapters, we will further explore advanced strategies for optimizing rewards, understanding the nuances of bonus offers, and intricacies around travel hacking that offer even greater rewards on your financial endeavors. With the right mindset and tools, cash back from your everyday spending can become a powerful ally in achieving your financial goals.

$$$$$$$$$

Chapter 5

Using Points and Miles Wisely

In today's world, savvy consumers can significantly reduce travel costs and enhance everyday purchases by harnessing the power of points and miles. Earning and redeeming these rewards efficiently can open doors to opportunities such as free flights, luxurious hotel stays, and memorable travel experiences. However, realizing the full potential of points and miles requires a strategic approach.

In this chapter, we will explore how to earn and redeem points and miles effectively while also outlining strategies for stretching their value to maximize your rewards.

How to Earn and Redeem Points and Miles Effectively

1. Understand the Earn Rates: Different credit cards and loyalty programs offer varied earn rates for points and miles. Understanding these rates is essential for effective accumulation:

Category Bonuses: Many travel and rewards cards provide enhanced earning rates in certain categories, such as dining, travel, groceries, or gas.

Identify which categories align with your spending and focus on accumulating points in these areas. For instance, a card that offers 3 points per dollar spent on travel and dining can yield significant rewards if you use it while incurring those expenses.

Sign-Up Bonuses: One of the most lucrative ways to boost your points balance is by taking advantage of sign-up bonuses when opening new credit cards. Many cards offer substantial rewards (for example, 50,000 points or more) after you meet the initial spending requirement. Strategically planning your spending during this period can provide a thrilling head start to your rewards journey.

Partnerships and Promotions: Many airlines and hotel chains partner with other businesses, allowing you to earn extra points or miles. Look out for promotional offers and check if your credit card has partnerships with retailers or service providers to accumulate points faster. For instance, using a co-branded airline credit card at certain hotels might offer bonus miles.

2. Take Advantage of Loyalty Programs: Sign up for loyalty programs associated with airlines, hotel chains, or other travel aggregators:

Enroll in Frequent Flyer Programs: Whenever you fly with an airline, it's beneficial to enroll in its frequent flyer program, even if you're not a frequent flyer. This allows you to accumulate miles that can be redeemed for future flights. The same applies to hotel loyalty programs, where you accumulate loyalty points that can be redeemed for free nights or upgrades.

Link Shopping Habits: Many airlines and hotel chains offer shopping portals where you can earn additional points by shopping with certain retailers. Linking your purchases to these portals can
provide extra points on purchases you were already planning to make.

Dining Partnerships and Promotions: Many loyalty programs have collaborations with restaurants where you can earn extra points for dining. Sign up for these partnerships to benefit from additional point accrual while enjoying a meal out.

3. Redeem Wisely: Once you have earned points or miles, it's time to think strategically about redeeming them:

Evaluate Redemption Options: When you're ready to redeem your points or miles, take the time to evaluate the different options available. Points can typically be redeemed for flights, hotel stays, car rentals, merchandise, or experiences. However, the value varies widely based on the redemption method. Flights and hotel stays often yield the highest redemption values compared to gift cards or merchandise.

Leverage Award Flights: Award flights usually offer the best value for miles. Check for availability and compare the miles required for different routes, dates, or times. Flexibility can lead to better deals. Use tools such as airline alliances to book multi-airline itineraries, potentially saving you significant miles.

Be Aware of Blackout Dates and Fees: When redeeming points or miles, be cognizant of blackout dates, associated fees, or additional costs (like fuel surcharges on award flights). Ensure you understand all terms before booking to maximize the value of your rewards.

Strategies for Stretching the Value of Points and Miles: To truly maximize the value of your points and miles, consider implementing the following strategies:

1. Be Flexible with Travel Dates and Locations: Flexibility can significantly enhance redemption opportunities:

Use Flexible Date Searches: When searching for flights or accommodations, use the "flexible dates" option available on many travel booking websites. This allows you to see the best value for points or miles across a range of dates, helping you identify ideal travel windows.

Consider Alternate Airports: If you live near more than one airport, explore flights from each airport. Sometimes, flying from a secondary airport can result in lower mileage costs, greater availability, or more favorable redemption options.

Explore Nearby Destinations: Look beyond your intended destination. Nearby cities may offer more reasonable mileage requirements or better availability for accommodations, allowing you to stretch your rewards further.

2. Utilize Points and Miles for Upgrades: Using points or miles for upgrades can enhance your travel experience:

Upgrade Your Seat: Consider using points or miles to upgrade your flight. Many airlines allow you to use accumulated points to move from economy to premium cabin seating, offering a more enjoyable travel experience without the full fare cost.

Hotel Room Upgrades: Some hotel loyalty programs allow for upgrades to better rooms or suites using points. If you're celebrating a special occasion or looking for extra comfort, we recommend redeeming points for an upgrade rather than just booking a standard room.

3. Engage in Travel Hacks: Exploit travel hacks to stretch your rewards creatively:

Book Round-Trip Flights: Sometimes booking a round-trip flight with miles can be cheaper than booking two one-way tickets, so always check both options before redeeming.

Free One-Way Award Tickets: Certain loyalty programs permit travelers to include free one-way trips on award tickets. For example, if you are booking a round-trip flight from your home to a destination, explore if you can add a one-way ticket back home afterward.

Use Airline Alliances: Take advantage of airline alliances to maximize your miles. For example, if your program is part of an alliance (like Star Alliance or Oneworld), you can use your miles across various airlines, expanding your travel options and availability of award seats.

4. Monitor Promotions and Loyalty Program Changes. Staying attuned to program promotions and changes can yield additional value:

Follow Loyalty Programs: Subscribe to newsletters or follow loyalty programs on social media to keep up with promotions, bonus offers, and changes. Occasionally, programs offer limited-time promotions that significantly boost point accrual rates or introduce new redemption opportunities.

Utilize All Available Channels: Sometimes, the same travel booking may require different amounts of points or miles across various channels (the airline's website, third-party travel sites, etc.). Always check where a flight or hotel redemption is the cheapest in terms of points.

5. Redeem Points for Experiences. Look beyond traditional redemptions and consider redeeming points for unique experiences:

Use Points for Events or Activities: Some loyalty programs allow points to be redeemed for concerts, fine dining experiences, or adventure activities. These experiences can often yield more joy than standard hotel or flight redemptions.

Charitable Donations: Some loyalty programs allow you to donate points or miles to charities. While not a direct financial benefit to you, it's an excellent way to give back and create a positive impact.

Mastering the art of using points and miles wisely can lead to fantastic travel opportunities and savings, transforming everyday purchases into adventures. By understanding how to earn points effectively, choosing the best redemption strategies, and stretching the value of your rewards through innovative tactics, you can make the most of your earned rewards.

Ultimately, the key to success lies in being informed, adaptable, and strategic. With careful planning and diligent management, you can leverage your points and miles to unlock extraordinary travel experiences that align with your budget and lifestyle.

As we continue to explore the nuances of credit card rewards in the following chapters, we will delve further into tips for optimizing travel arrangements, navigating loyalty programs, and additional strategies for ensuring that your points and miles continue to reward you generously long into the future.

$$$$$$$$$

Chapter 6
Understanding Transfer Partners

In the world of frequent flyer programs and loyalty rewards, one of the most powerful strategies for maximizing the value of your points and miles is understanding and utilizing transfer partners. Many credit card companies and loyalty programs offer opportunities to transfer points to various airline and hotel partners, allowing you to unlock significant value in your travel experiences.

In this chapter, we will delve into the benefits of transferring points, how to identify and approach these partners, and strategies for maximizing value through strategic point transfers.

Benefits of Transferring Points to Airline and Hotel Partners. Understanding the mechanics and benefits of transferring points can significantly enhance your travel options, giving you access to premium flights, luxurious accommodations, and exclusive experiences. Here are some key benefits of transferring points to airline and hotel partners:

1. Unlock Enhanced Redemption Opportunities: Transferring points to loyalty programs can unlock exclusive redemption opportunities that would not be available if you redeemed points directly from your credit card issuer:

Higher Value Redemptions: Oftentimes, transferring points to an airline or hotel partner can yield better redemption value than straightforward cash back or merchandise redemptions. For instance, using travel points for flights can sometimes provide much more value per point than redeeming those same points for a gift card.

Access to Award Flights: Many airlines offer award tickets only to frequent flyer program members. By transferring points from your credit card, you gain access to these valuable tickets, which can include discounted award flights, cabin upgrades, and availability for popular routes.

2. Opportunity for Miles and Points Bonuses: Engaging in point transfers to certain airline and hotel partners can sometimes come with additional bonuses:

Transfer Bonuses: Credit card companies or loyalty programs occasionally run promotions offering bonus points or miles for transfers to specific partners. If you wait for these promotions, you can maximize the amount you earn in each transfer, compounding the value you receive.

Accelerate Your Earnings: When transferring points during a promotional period, you can achieve your travel goals quicker. For example, transferring points that give you an additional 30% can be the difference between getting a flight ticket now versus waiting months to gather more points.

3. Greater Flexibility and Options: Frequent travelers often benefit from the flexibility offered by transferring points:

Leverage Alliances and Partnerships: Many airlines and hotel chains are connected through alliances, allowing you to transfer points across various partners. This interconnectedness opens a wide array of travel opportunities, helping you navigate around fewer available award flights or hotels.

Pick the Best Deals: With the ability to transfer points among various partners, you can pick the best route for your travels. For instance, utilizing a mix of airline networks offers more choices for flights and optimal redemption options that fit your schedule.

4. Tailored Travel Experiences: Transferring points provides the opportunity to tailor your travel experiences according to your preferences:

Optimize Travel Plans: For travelers who have specific destinations or lodgings in mind, transferring points to a preferred hotel chain or airline can give you access to great options that fit your plans perfectly.

Personalized Upgrades and Benefits: Some loyalty programs allow members to redeem points for upgrades, such as room upgrades at hotels or premium seating on flights. By transferring points, you customize your experiences, turning a standard trip into an exceptional one.

Maximizing Value Through Strategic Point Transfers

While the benefits of transferring points to partners are clear, strategically doing so requires a thoughtful approach. Here are some strategies to ensure you're maximizing the value of your point transfers:

1. Research and Understand Airline and Hotel Partners: Before transferring points, conduct thorough research to understand the various partners associated with your loyalty program. Assess each partner's requirements and options:

Review Award Charts: Many airline loyalty programs publish award charts that outline how many miles are needed for a particular flight or upgrade. Frequent analysis of travel routes and prices can guide you to the most rewarding transfer opportunities.

Evaluate Partners: Different hotel chains and airlines have varying qualities. Research potential partners to determine which offer the best value and benefits based on your travel preferences. Are they known for good customer service? Do they offer decent lounge access or room upgrades to frequent flyers? A deeper understanding will help you make more informed transfer decisions.

2. Think About the Transfer Ratio: Pay attention to the point transfer ratios before moving points between programs:

Transfer Rates: Understand how many points/miles you will receive in the partner program relative to how many you are transferring. Different programs have varied transfer rates (e.g., 1:1, 2:1) that can impact your decision on whether to proceed.

Calculate Value: Use your research to calculate the potential value of your points once transferred. If an airline partner requires 25,000 points for an award flight that would typically cost 1,000 points through your credit card program, it may not be worth the transfer.

3. Use Points for Desired Experiences: Once you've identified the points conversion that offers the best value, plan to redeem points effectively:

Book in Advance: Award flights and hotel stays can be scarce, especially during peak travel seasons. Booking your rewards well in advance will generally, provide more availability and lower your risk of missing out on a great deal.

Maximize Transferred Points: When you know you need a specific number of points for a booking, calculate how many to transfer and when it will be most advantageous to do so. This will help you avoid transferring too many points or losing out on better transfer bonuses later.

4. Monitor Promotions and Changes: Keep an eye on loyalty programs and credit card companies for promotions:

Transfer Promotions: Check for promotional periods and bonuses. Being proactive about transferring points during these times can dramatically increase the value you receive from your points.

Stay Updated with Program Changes: Loyalty programs frequently alter their terms, transfer rates, and redemption opportunities. Be sure to monitor any changes to ensure you maintain maximum value for your points and miles.

5. Diversify Your Points Earning: Expand your point-earning strategies to include multiple loyalty programs:

Utilize Multiple Rewards Programs: If you earn points across various credit cards and hotel or airline programs, you can enjoy greater transfer flexibility. This approach allows you to aggregate points in one program for enhanced value, depending on your travel plans.

Limit Accumulation in One Program: While concentrating points in one loyalty program can feel beneficial, it's often wiser to manage points across several programs. This strategy helps to anticipate valuable transfer opportunities as they arise.

Understanding and leveraging transfer partners can elevate your travel rewards experience significantly. By effectively transferring points to airline and hotel partners, you unlock unparalleled potential for enhanced travel options, better redemption value, and exciting upgrades.

By engaging in diligent research, calculating your transfer ratios carefully, monitoring promotions, and diversifying your point-earning strategies, you can champion the effective use of your points and miles. As you continue exploring the world of travel rewards, the subsequent chapters will delve further into maximizing specific programs, understanding loyalty strategies, and tips for utilizing points for unforgettable travel experiences. Remember, the art of transferring points lies not just in the transfer itself, but in the thoughtful approach you take toward managing and redeeming them to create memories that last a lifetime.

$$$$$$$$$

Chapter 7

Utilizing Introductory 0% APR Offers

In an era where interest rates can significantly affect financial decisions, understanding and utilizing credit card offers that include 0% APR (annual percentage rate) for an introductory period can be a smart move for savvy consumers. This chapter explores how you can make the most of these offers, whether for big purchases, travel plans, or balance transfers, while also delving into important strategies for avoiding pitfalls when the introductory period comes to a close.

How to Use 0% APR Offers for Big Purchases or Balance Transfers

1. Understanding 0% APR Offers: 0% APR offers are promotional rates extended by credit card issuers for a set period, typically ranging from 6 to 18 months, depending on the card. During this period, you can carry a balance without accruing interest, making these offers especially appealing for large purchases or consolidating debt.

Big Purchases

Large Expenses: When planning significant purchases, such as home renovations, major appliances, or a family vacation, a 0% APR offer can provide immediate purchasing power without the burden of interest payments. Instead of paying with cash or incurring high-interest debt, you can spread the cost over several months with no interest charge.

Budgeting Strategy: Use the interest-free period to budget effectively. For example, if you make a $3,000 purchase with a 12-month 0% APR offer, this translates to monthly payments of $250. Setting up a structured payment plan ensures that you can pay off the balance before the promotional period ends.

Balance Transfers

Debt Consolidation: If you're carrying balances on high-interest credit cards, transferring that debt to a new card with a 0% APR offer is an excellent strategy. This can save you significant amounts in interest charges and help accelerate your debt repayment.

Calculate Transfer Fees: Be mindful that most credit cards charge a balance transfer fee, typically around 3% to 5% of the transferred amount. Before committing, calculate whether the savings from interest payments will outweigh these fees. For instance, if you're transferring a $10,000 balance with a 3% fee, you'd incur a $300 charge. Balance this fee against the interest savings to determine if it's a worthwhile move.

2. Planning for Payments: For both big purchases and balance transfers, having a solid plan in place for repayment is essential:

Set a Reminder: Mark your calendar with the date the introductory period ends to avoid surprises. If you haven't paid off the balance by this date, any remaining amount will begin accruing interest at the regular rate, which may be significantly higher.

Establish Automatic Payments: Set up automatic payments equal to or greater than the minimum due each month. This strategy helps ensure you maintain good standing with your issuer, build positive credit history, and avoid missed payments.

Monitor Your Spending: Just because you have access to a promotional interest rate doesn't mean you should overextend yourself. Continue to keep track of your overall financial health and expenditures, staying within a budget that allows you to pay down your debt effectively.

Avoiding Pitfalls When the Introductory Period Ends: While introductory 0% APR offers can be advantageous, a lack of planning can lead to costly mistakes once the promotional period concludes. Here are several strategies to avoid common pitfalls:

1. Know Your Card's Terms: Read the Fine Print: Each credit card has specific terms and conditions regarding the interest rate that takes effect after the promotional period ends. Some cards have variable rates, meaning your interest rate could fluctuate based on market conditions. Be aware of your card's regular APR and any applicable fees.

Understand APR Increases: If you miss a payment during the promotional period, the lender may revoke the 0% APR offer and revert to charging interest at a higher standard rate. Always ensure timely monthly payments to maintain your promotional rate.

2. Create a Payoff Strategy

Calculate Your Payoff Amount: Before the promotional period ends, take a close look at your balance and determine how much you still owe. Create a detailed payment plan, establishing how much you need to pay each month to eliminate your balance before interest kicks in.

Prioritize High-Interest Debt: If you have multiple credit card balances, consider applying any extra payments towards the balance that carries the highest interest rate. This approach not only helps you clear your debt quicker but also reduces the total interest paid in the long run.

3. Prepare for the End of the Introductory Period: Avoid New Purchases: Once you've utilized a 0% APR offer, focus on paying down the debt associated with the initial purchase or balance transfer. Adding new transactions to a card can complicate your repayment plan and put you at risk of accumulating more debt.

Consider Your Next Steps: As you approach the end of the promotional period, assess your options. If you have not paid off your entire balance, consider transferring your remaining balance to another card that offers a new 0% APR promotion, if it's feasible and cost-effective.

4. Monitor Your Credit Utilization

Impact on Credit Score: The balance you carry relative to your credit limit significantly affects your credit score. As your balance increases due to new purchases or remaining debt, monitor your credit utilization to ensure it remains within healthy limits (generally below 30% of your total credit limit).

Use Alerts and Notifications: Utilize your credit card issuer's mobile app or website to set alerts for payment due dates, spending thresholds, or remaining credits. Staying informed can help you manage your credit responsibly.

Introductory 0% APR offers can be a powerful tool for managing big purchases or consolidating high-interest debt, providing financial flexibility in a variety of situations. However, it's essential to approach these offers with a clear strategy and an awareness of the potential pitfalls once the promotional period ends.

By understanding the terms of these offers, planning your payments effectively, and maintaining vigilance about your spending habits, you can leverage 0% APR offers to your advantage. Ultimately, informed decision-making and disciplined repayment strategies can lead you not only to financial relief but also to enhancing your overall credit score and financial health.

With each new tool and technique, you'll be better equipped to make informed decisions that work for you, fostering a healthier financial journey in the long term.

$$$$$$$$

Chapter 8

Combining Multiple Cards for Optimal Rewards

In the realm of credit card rewards, one of the most effective strategies to maximize benefits is to strategically combine multiple cards to suit your spending habits and lifestyle. Credit cards come with various rewards structures, including cash back, points, and miles, which can be tailored to your specific needs.

This chapter will explore tips for using multiple cards, how to create a spending strategy that takes advantage of category-specific rewards, and a framework for maximizing benefits across your entire portfolio of cards.

Tips for Using Multiple Cards to Maximize Benefits: Using multiple credit cards can seem daunting at first, but it can significantly enhance your rewards potential. Here are actionable tips for effectively leveraging multiple cards:

1. Assess Your Spending Habits: Before you begin applying for different cards, take the time to analyze your monthly spending:

Track Your Expenses: Understanding where you spend the most will help you identify which categories and types of cards will yield the best rewards. Common categories include grocery stores, dining out, travel expenses, gas, and online shopping.

Create a Budget: Establishing a budget can also help you allocate your spending appropriately across different cards. This foundational step will ensure you're not overspending just to earn rewards, which could lead to debt.

2. Choose Cards with Different Reward Structures: Different credit cards offer varying rewards based on spending categories and overall structure:

Categorical Cards: Some cards specialize in particular categories—like 5% cash back on groceries or dining—while others offer a flat rate for all purchases. By combining a categorical card with a general rewards card, you can maximize the potential for points or cash back.

Sign-Up Bonuses: When selecting new cards, consider those that offer significant sign-up bonuses. These bonuses can provide a substantial rewards boost, especially if you can meet the spending requirement during the introductory period.

3. Leverage Loyalty Programs: If you travel frequently, consider cards tied to airline or hotel loyalty programs:

Tiered Benefits: Some travel rewards credit cards provide benefits that can elevate the rewards you earn, such as priority boarding on flights or hotel upgrades. Combine these with general spend cards to ensure you're maximizing every dollar spent, even when you aren't traveling.

Transfer Points: Using a combination of cards that allow you to transfer points to travel partners can further enhance your rewards. For example, points from a general rewards card can be transferred to an airline loyalty program for use towards award flights.

4. Stay Organized with Payment Dates: Using multiple credit cards means keeping track of payment dates to avoid late fees and interest charges:

Use Calendar Alerts: Set up calendar reminders for payment due dates, and consider synchronizing your bills to allow for streamlined payments. This step helps avoid any adverse effects on your credit score due to missed payments.

Automate Payments: If possible, consider setting up automatic payments for at least the minimum balance due. This ensures you maintain your account in good standing, especially if you have multiple cards.

5. Review Benefits and Rewards Regularly: Keeping up with changes in credit card rewards and benefits can help you adjust your strategy as needed:

Stay Informed: Credit card companies regularly update rewards programs and benefits. Make a habit of reviewing your cards once or twice a year to find out if they still align with your spending patterns. A card that was beneficial last year may not offer the best value anymore.

Maintain Flexibility: If a current card isn't meeting your needs, don't hesitate to explore new options. Many credit card issuers provide promotional offers to attract new customers, so keep your options open for the best potential rewards.

Creating a Strategy for Category and General Spending: A successful rewards strategy hinges on a well-thought-out plan that accounts for both category-specific and general spending. Here are actionable steps to create an effective rewards strategy:

1. Identify Category Spending Opportunities: Understanding which spending categories align with your lifestyle is crucial. Here's how to maximize category rewards:

Categorical Analysis: Start by calculating how much you spend in each category monthly. Break your expenses down into key categories, such as groceries, dining, gas, clothing, and travel.

Match Cards to Categories: After identifying your highest spending categories, align them with cards that offer the best rewards for those specific areas. For example, if you frequently dine out, choose a card that offers enhanced rewards in the dining category.

2. Utilize General Reward Cards for Everyday Purchases: While categorical spending is essential, use general rewards cards for overall purchases:

Flat Rewards Cards: Consider a credit card that offers a flat rate of rewards on all purchases. This can be beneficial for handling miscellaneous expenses or when spending in categories that don't have a designated higher reward card.

Supplement with Category Cards: When making purchases that don't fall within your high-reward categories, use a flat-rate card for simplicity and efficiency. This ensures that no spending opportunity is wasted.

3. Utilize Rotating Categories: Some rewards cards offer rotating category bonuses, changing quarterly or annually:

Stay Ahead of the Game: Familiarize yourself with these rotating categories and plan your spending around them. If a card offers 5% cash back on home improvement stores for a quarter, consider timing any planned renovations or purchases accordingly.

Opt for Sign-Up Bonuses: If you're considering applying for a new card, check whether it has a rotating category for the sign-up bonus. You could potentially maximize both the bonus and category rewards in the same period.

4. Create a Calendar or Spreadsheet: To further streamline your rewards strategy, create a visual guide:

Rewards Calendar: Construct a simple calendar or spreadsheet that outlines your cards' rewards categories, bonus opportunities, and any relevant expiration dates for points. This visual aid can help you organize your spending accordingly, maximizing your rewards potential.

Recording Spending: You can also record your actual spending in various categories to ensure you are achieving the expected rewards. Tracking your purchases will allow you to adjust future spending in real-time.

5. Evaluate and Adjust: Once you have your strategy in place, regularly evaluate its effectiveness:

Assess Realignment Needs: After a few months, review how well you're accumulating rewards against your goals. If you find that you're not maximizing your cards' benefits, consider realigning your spending habits with your chosen cards.

Adapt to Life Changes: Life circumstances such as changing jobs, relocating, or new family members can impact spending habits. Remain adaptable and adjust your strategy as necessary to align with any changes in your lifestyle.

6. Maximize Point Transfers and Redemptions: Finally, utilize points and rewards efficiently:

Timing of Usage: Make strategic decisions about when to redeem points or cash back. Look for opportunities to use points during promotions or special occasions when redemption values may be higher.

Use the Right Card for Redemption: When redeeming awards, consider using a card that offers additional bonuses for travel-related expenses, ensuring that your spend equates to additional value back into your rewards account.

Combining multiple credit cards strategically can lead to a robust rewards system that maximizes benefits across various categories and everyday spending. By assessing your habits, leveraging the right rewards cards, and staying organized with your payment plans, you can enrich your rewards experience while maintaining financial responsibility.

As you implement a strategy to optimize category rewards and general spending, be open to reevaluating and adjusting your approach based on changing spending habits and new card offers. The ability to adapt will keep you engaged in the process, and over time, your diligence will pay off in the form of valuable rewards, created memories from travel, or those little luxuries that come from careful financial planning.

With a well-rounded understanding and a robust strategy, you can tap into the full potential of your credit cards to create rewarding experiences while navigating the credit landscape with confidence.

$$$$$$$$$

Chapter 9

Exploiting Quarterly and Annual Category Bonuses

In the world of credit card rewards, quarterly and annual category bonuses present golden opportunities to maximize your return on spending. Many credit cards offer enhanced rewards in designated categories for specific periods, allowing cardholders to earn higher cash back or points on particular types of purchases. This chapter will explore strategies for tracking and utilizing these bonus categories effectively. We'll also discuss best practices for setting reminders to ensure you never miss out on a valuable rewards opportunity.

Tracking and Utilizing Bonus Categories

1. Understanding Bonus Categories: Before diving into the strategies for tracking and utilizing bonus categories, it's essential to understand what they are:

Quarterly Categories: Many cards offer rotating categories that change every three months. These categories can include specific merchants or general areas such as grocery stores, gas stations, or dining. During the promotional period, users earn a higher percentage of rewards, often 5%, for spending on eligible purchases.

Annual Categories: Some cards feature annual bonuses that are consistent throughout the year or specific to certain spending behaviors, such as airline purchases or hotel stays. These cards often come with a cap on the amount of spending that qualifies for the elevated rewards rate.

2. Keeping a Record of Bonus Categories: To take full advantage of category bonuses, maintaining an organized record is crucial. Here are some tips to help you keep track:

Create a Category Calendar: Develop a simple calendar that outlines when bonus categories change and the specific categories themselves. This visual representation can help you adjust your spending habits accordingly. You can use a paper calendar, an app, or a spreadsheet based on your preferences.

For example, your calendar may look like this:

Quarter	Bonus Category
Q1	Grocery stores
Q2	Gas and travel
Q3	Restaurants
Q4	Online shopping

Utilize Financial Apps: Many budgeting and expenditure tracking apps allow you to categorize purchases and set reminders. Using an app can streamline tracking and help you remember the bonus categories more effectively.

Review Card Issuer Promotions: Regularly check your card issuer's website or app for updates on bonuses and promotional periods. This practice ensures you're up-to-date and can adjust your card usage as necessary for the most beneficial spending patterns.

3. Plan Your Spending Around Bonus Categories: With knowledge of the current and upcoming bonus categories, strategize your spending to maximize rewards:

Adjust Your Purchasing Order: If you know certain categories are coming up, consider postponing purchases until the category bonus activates. For instance, if you see that groceries will have a bonus next quarter, plan to stock up then rather than during a non-bonus period.

Group Your Purchases: Whenever practical, consolidate your spending in the bonus category during the promotional period. For example, if the bonus category is gas, make an effort to fill up your tank or purchase any necessary fuel accessories all at once rather than spreading them out over the quarter.

4. Optimize Category Spending for Large Purchases: Bonus categories can also relate to larger expenses, making them an excellent opportunity for maximizing your rewards:

Timing Large Purchases: If you anticipate making a significant purchase, such as home improvements or electronics, try to time it with the relevant bonus category. It can turn a regular expense into rewards-earning behavior.

Utilize Multiple Cards: If you have more than one card that offers rotating rewards, take advantage of category overlaps. For example, if you have two cards with a bonus on grocery spending during the same quarter, split your spending between them to enhance the benefits.

Setting Reminders to Activate Rotating Categories: Missing out on activating rotating categories can be a costly mistake for anyone relying on credit card rewards. Ensuring you are organized and timely is crucial to capturing every bonus opportunity. Here's how to do that effectively:

1. **Understanding Activation Requirements:** First, always read the terms surrounding category bonuses:

Activation Requirements: Some cards require activation to earn the enhanced rewards. This requirement is commonly associated with rotating categories, where you must log in to your account to activate the promotion.

Deadlines: Be aware of the activation deadlines, as some issuers may limit the timeframe for activation at the beginning of a new quarter.

2. Use Calendar Alerts and Reminders: Setting up reminders can help you stay on top of rotating categories:

Digital Calendar Alerts: Utilize a digital calendar (e.g., Google Calendar, Outlook) to set recurring reminders. For example, create an alert two weeks before the end of each quarter to remind yourself to activate the next quarter's categories. You might also set a reminder for a few days before a quarter starts to remind you of the new categories.

Smartphone Reminders: Use your smartphone's reminder feature to set notifications for key activation dates. You could even set reminders on the days leading up to the start of a new quarter.

3. Engage with Mobile Apps: Many credit card issuers provide mobile apps that allow you to manage your account more efficiently:

Push Notifications: Enable push notifications on your credit card app to receive continuous updates about upcoming promotions and bonuses. This can streamline your process and ensure you never miss an opportunity.

Tracking Functions: Some apps provide functions for tracking your spending patterns and automatically notifying you when you're nearing the end of a promotional period or when bonus categories are about to change.

4. Create a Physical Calendar or Planner: If you prefer analog methods, consider designing a physical planner or calendar for tracking your credit card bonuses:

Bi-weekly Review: Dedicate a specific time, such as every two weeks, to check your calendar against your spending and credit card promotions. Use this time to activate categories and strategize for the following weeks.

Color Coding: Use color-coded sticky notes or markers in your planner to denote different credit card categories. These visual cues will enhance your awareness of which cards to use depending on the time of the year.

5. Leverage Email Alerts: Set up email alerts from your card issuer:

Sign Up for Notifications: Sign up for email notifications about rewards promotions, bonus categories, and necessary activation reminders. This proactive approach ensures you receive timely reminders right to your inbox.

Subscription Management: Keep an organized email folder for all your credit card-related correspondence, helping you quickly locate important information about category bonuses and rewards programs.

Exploiting quarterly and annual category bonuses can greatly enhance your rewards-earning potential, transforming everyday spending into significant benefits. By tracking bonus categories diligently, adapting your spending strategies, and setting reminders for activation, you can ensure that you make the most of every opportunity that arises.

As you strategize around rotating bonuses, remember that organizational skills and planning are critical. With diligent tracking, timely activation, and purposeful spending, you can navigate the complexities of credit card rewards with confidence and ease.

As we continue this exploration, we'll further explore the world of credit card rewards, providing insights into maximizing travel rewards, understanding the mechanics of loyalty points, and developing long-term strategies to enrich your financial future. With each new strategy, you'll be better prepared to leverage the power of credit card rewards to enhance your lifestyle, create memorable experiences, and strengthen your financial health.

$$$$$$$$$

Chapter 10

Travel Perks and Benefits

Travel is one of life's greatest joys, but it can also be laden with hidden costs and unexpected inconveniences. Fortunately, many credit cards, and loyalty programs, offer a variety of travel perks and benefits that can greatly enhance your experience while minimizing expenses. From no foreign transaction fees to travel insurance and lounge access, understanding these advantages is essential for any savvy traveler. In this chapter, we will delve into the most common travel perks associated with credit cards, explore how to maximize lounge access, baggage benefits, and upgrades, and offer practical

tips for leveraging these advantages to elevate your travel experience.

Understanding Common Travel Perks: Before you embark on your journey, it's crucial to familiarize yourself with the common travel perks that can enhance your overall travel experience. Here are some key benefits provided by many travel-focused credit cards:

1. No Foreign Transaction Fees: One of the most significant perks of certain credit cards is the elimination of foreign transaction fees:

What It Is: Many credit cards impose a fee, usually around 3%, for transactions processed outside the home country. When traveling internationally, these fees can quickly add up, making your purchases more expensive.

How to Benefit: Look for credit cards designed for travelers that waive foreign transaction fees. This way, you can use your card abroad without incurring additional costs for every purchase. It can also be safer than carrying large sums of cash in foreign currencies.

2. Travel Insurance: Travel insurance is essential for protecting against unforeseen circumstances that can disrupt your trip:

Types of Coverage: Many travel reward cards offer varying degrees of travel insurance, which may include trip cancellation, trip interruption, baggage delay, and emergency medical assistance. Even a minor delay could lead to extra costs for accommodation or missed connections.

How to Leverage It: Before booking your next trip, review the travel insurance policy that comes with your credit card. Understand the coverage limits and any requirements, such as using the card for travel purchases to activate coverage. This proactive approach can provide peace of mind while traveling.

3. Rental Car Benefits: For those planning to rent a vehicle during their travels, certain credit cards provide useful perks:

Collision Damage Waiver (CDW): Many cards include CDW insurance when you use the card to pay for your rental, eliminating or reducing the need for expensive rental company insurance. This can save you money while providing coverage for damages.

How to Use This Benefit: Always review the terms and conditions before relying on your credit card's rental car insurance. It's important to understand the coverage limits and ensure that you decline additional insurance offered by the rental agency.

4. Concierge Services: High-tier travel credit cards often provide concierge services that can add a level of convenience to your travel experience:

What They Offer: Depending on your card, concierge services can help with travel planning, restaurant reservations, and securing event tickets. Some services can assist in unique experiences, such as guided tours or exclusive access to venues.

Maximizing the Service: Familiarize yourself with the available concierge services and don't hesitate to make use of them when planning trips. Whether you need help finding a local restaurant or booking last-minute accommodations, concierge teams can make your trip smoother.

Maximizing Lounge Access, Baggage Benefits, and Upgrades: Understanding how to leverage travel perks is essential for getting the most value from them. Here's how to maximize benefits like lounge access, checked baggage, and upgrades:

1. Lounge Access: Airport lounges provide a more comfortable and relaxed atmosphere to wait for your flight:

Types of Lounges: There are several types of lounges, including those operated by airlines, affiliated lounge networks (such as Priority Pass), and credit card issuers. Each offers different amenities, ranging from complimentary food and drinks to business services.

How to Access: Many travel credit cards offer complimentary lounge access or memberships with certain lounges. Take advantage of these offerings by planning your arrivals early to enjoy the benefits. For instance, if you have priority access to a lounge through your card, arrive at the airport with enough time to unwind before your flight.

Guest Policies: Be aware of each lounge's guest policy. Some lounges allow you to bring guests for free or at a reduced rate. If you're traveling with friends or family, this can significantly enhance your pre-flight experience, allowing everyone to enjoy the benefits of the lounge.

2. Baggage Benefits: Checked baggage fees can eat into your travel budget, but certain credit cards offer ways to alleviate these costs:

Free Checked Bags: Many airline-affiliated credit cards provide one or two free checked bags for cardholders and often their companions traveling on the same reservation. This perk can save you a significant amount (up to $60 per round trip) depending on the airline.

Priority Boarding: Several travel cards also provide priority boarding benefits, enabling cardholders to get on the plane early and secure overhead bin space for their carry-on luggage. This can create a less stressful boarding experience.

Maximizing Benefits: To make the most of checked baggage benefits, ensure you use the card to purchase your airline tickets to activate the perks. Keep in mind the policies regarding companions traveling with you to fully utilize these savings.

3. Upgrades: Travel upgrades can transform your journey, providing more comfort whether you're on a long-haul flight or a short domestic trip:

Types of Upgrades: Upgrades can include moving from economy to business class or obtaining extra legroom in premium seating. Some cards offer complimentary upgrades or allow you to use points for upgrades.

Best Practices for Securing Upgrades: To increase your chances of scoring an upgrade, consider the following strategies:

Fly During Off-Peak Times: Traveling during less busy times of the day or week can improve your chances of an available upgrade since flights may be less crowded.

Join Loyalty Programs: Being a loyal customer with an airline can help secure better upgrade opportunities. Many cards also give bonus loyalty points when you book travel through the issuer.

Inquire at Check-In: Don't hesitate to ask about potential upgrades politely at check-in or when you board. Sometimes staff can offer upgrades if available, and your friendly demeanor can work in your favor.

Using Points for Upgrades: Many cards allow you to use accrued points or miles for upgrades. If you have a significant points balance, strategically planning the use of these points for premium seating upgrades can provide an enhanced travel experience.

Additional Travel Perks to Consider: Apart from the aforementioned benefits, several other travel perks can enhance your travel experience:

1. **Travel Assistance Services:** Some premium cards offer robust travel assistance services

in case of emergencies while traveling, which can be invaluable:

Emergency Assistance: Services may include legal referrals, lost luggage assistance, and medical referrals. Having access to these services can provide peace of mind during your travels.

2. Global Entry/TSA PreCheck Credits: Frequent travelers can benefit from expedited security screening through Global Entry or TSA PreCheck programs:

Program Benefits: These programs allow you to bypass long security lines at airports, making travel more efficient. Many premium travel cards offer a statement credit for application fees, effectively covering the costs for cardholders.

3. No Blackout Dates on Rewards Travel: Some credit cards offer travel rewards that can be redeemed without blackout dates, allowing for greater flexibility in planning your trips:

Flexible Redemption: This feature gives you the ability to book flights or hotel rooms even during peak travel times when other loyalty programs may impose restrictions.

Understanding and maximizing travel perks and benefits can take your travel experience from ordinary to extraordinary. From avoiding foreign transaction fees and protecting your travel investments with insurance to enjoying the comforts of airport lounges and taking advantage of baggage allowances and upgrades, the right travel credit card can truly enrich your journeys.

As you plan your next trip, make sure to review the specific travel benefits offered by your credit cards. Utilize everything from lounge access to travel insurance to ensure a seamless experience. Each perk can contribute to a more enjoyable and cost-effective journey.

Whether you aspire to jet around the world in business class, embark on adventurous trips, or make
the most of your loyalty programs, navigating the landscape of credit card perks will equip you with the knowledge needed to travel wisely and comfortably. With careful planning and a strategic approach, your
travels can yield unforgettable memories and meaningful experiences well beyond the destinations you visit.

$$$$$$$$$

Chapter 11
Dining and Grocery Rewards

When it comes to maximizing your credit card rewards, dining and grocery purchases represent significant opportunities. These essential spending categories often make up a substantial portion of everyday expenses, and many credit cards offer robust rewards programs that allow consumers to earn cashback or points. In this chapter, we'll dive deep into how to identify credit cards that excel in dining and grocery rewards and explore strategies to maximize your earnings on these essential expenditures.

Identifying Cards with Strong Dining and Grocery Rewards: Selecting the right credit card for dining and grocery purchases is critical for maximizing rewards. Here are the types of cards you should consider as you evaluate your options.

1. Cashback Credit Cards: Cashback credit cards typically offer straightforward rewards systems, allowing you to earn a percentage of your spend back on your purchases. Many of these cards feature enhanced rates for grocery and dining expenses.

Typical Offers: Look for cards that offer 3%-6% cash back on dining and grocery purchases. Some cards might specify a maximum spending limit for the elevated cash back rate per quarter, and others may define categories that change monthly or quarterly.

Examples:

Capital One SavorOne Cash Rewards: This card offers 3% cash back on dining and entertainment, as well as grocery purchases. It also has no annual fee, making it appealing for casual spending.

Citi Double Cash Card: While it doesn't have a tiered reward structure, it offers 2% cash back on all purchases, 1% when you buy and 1% when you pay for your balance. This rewards flexibility can be useful for frequent diners and grocery shoppers.

2. Rewards Credit Cards: Rewards credit cards, often associated with travel or hotel loyalty programs, can provide points for themes aligned with your habits, such as dining and grocery shopping.

Understanding Points Multipliers: Many credit cards in this category provide points multipliers for certain types of spending, including dining and groceries. This means you can earn additional points for every dollar spent in these categories.

Examples:

Chase Sapphire Preferred: Offers 2x points on dining and travel, making it a strong contender for anyone who frequently dines out or travels.

American Express Gold Card: This card provides 4x points at restaurants, including takeout and delivery, and 3x points on flights booked directly with airlines or on amextravel.com.

3. Tiered Rewards Cards: Some credit cards feature tiered rewards, where you earn different rates depending on the total spending level achieved throughout the year.

How They Work: These cards may offer enhanced rewards in categories such as groceries and dining, with the possibility of earning more as you reach specific spending thresholds.

Examples:

Discover it® Cash Back: This card rotates categories every quarter, often focusing on grocery stores and dining. You can earn 5% cash back in those categories up to a specified limit when activated.

4. Co-Branded Cards: Co-branded credit cards are issued by banks in partnership with a specific retailer or restaurant chain. These cards often provide lucrative rewards for spending within a specific ecosystem.

How to Use Them: If you often dine at specific restaurants or grocery store chains, consider their co-branded cards. While they might typically offer lower rewards in non-affiliated establishments, the benefits can be significant where you spend the most.

Examples:

Starbucks Rewards Visa Card: Earns points on Starbucks purchases and provides additional points for dining at restaurants.

Target RedCard: Provides 5% off on purchases made at Target, including groceries, and no annual fee.

How to Earn Cashback or Points on Essential Spending: Now that you have identified credit cards with strong dining and grocery rewards, let's delve into strategies to maximize your cashback or points on essential spending effectively.

1. Strategic Spending

a. Use the Right Card for Each Purchase: To maximize rewards, it's critical to use the optimal card for each purchase:

Segment Your Spending: If you have several cards that offer rewards in different categories, create a plan to use your cards strategically based on where you're shopping. For groceries, for example, if one card offers a higher cash back rate at supermarkets, make sure to use that card for all grocery purchases.

b. Pay Attention to Rotating Categories

Activate Bonus Categories: If you have a card with rotating categories, ensure you activate them ahead of time. The Discover it® Cash Back card, for example, highlights grocery and dining categories at different times in the year, thus enabling you to maximize rewards during those quarters.

2. Take Advantage of Promotions and Offers

Limited-Time Offers: Be on the lookout for limited-time promotions from your card issuer. Many banks run temporary promotions where you can earn extra points or cash back on dining or grocery spending.

Dining Programs: Some credit cards are partnered with dining programs, providing extra rewards when you eat at participating restaurants.

Sign up for these programs and take advantage of any offers available.

3. Utilize Online Shopping Portals

Earning Points Online: Before shopping at grocery stores or dining establishments, check online shopping portals affiliated with your credit card to see if there are additional points or cashback opportunities for orders placed online.

Incorporate Grocery Delivery Services: If you prefer the convenience of grocery delivery, use your rewards card for online purchases through platforms like Instacart or Amazon Fresh, both of which often offer cashback or points for using certain credit cards.

4. Family Accounts and Shared Spending

a. Maximize Family Spending

Combine Spending: If you live with family or roommates, consider a joint strategy where everyone uses the same card for shared expenses—especially groceries. This approach amplifies your spending volume, yielding more rewards.

b. Adding Authorized Users

Additional Card Benefits: Adding approved users to your credit card account can allow them to earn points on purchases made with your card. It can be particularly beneficial if you want to amplify your rewards balance.

5. Keep Track of Your Rewards

Tracking Apps: Use budgeting and expense tracking applications that help consolidate your purchases and rewards into one hub, allowing you to see where you earn the most points or cash back.

Monitor Your Accounts: Regularly review your credit card statements and rewards dashboard to ensure you earn the advertised rewards. Awareness of your spending will also help you strategize future purchases.

6. Redeeming Rewards

Efficient Redemption: Always familiarize yourself with the redemption options available for your card. Depending on the structure, you may find better value in redeeming points for specific categories, like travel or cashback, which can supplement your future spending adventures.

Combining Rewards Programs: If possible, look into programs that allow you to transfer points between loyalty systems. This strategy can maximize value and flexibility for travel, dining experiences, or everyday expenses.

Dining and grocery rewards represent a prime opportunity to enhance your credit card rewards strategy. By identifying cards with strong offerings in these essential spending categories, you can significantly increase your cash back or points accumulation on purchases that you likely make regularly. By using the right card for the right purchases, strategically planning your spending, capitalizing on promotions, and monitoring your rewards, you can emerge as a savvy consumer with substantial returns on everyday expenses.

As you explore your dining preferences and grocery spending habits, remember that diligent planning and informed card usage are key to maximizing your rewards potential.

In the succeeding chapters, we'll continue to explore how different types of purchases can yield significant rewards, including travel, entertainment, and online shopping. With each area you master, you'll become increasingly adept at leveraging credit card rewards to enrich your financial life and enhance everyday experiences.

$$$$$$$$$

Chapter 12

Maximizing Online Shopping Rewards

In today's digital age, online shopping has become a staple for consumers around the globe. With the ability to access millions of products at the click of a button, it's no wonder that more and more people are turning to e-commerce for their shopping needs. But beyond the convenience and variety that online shopping offers, there's a powerful opportunity to maximize your rewards through credit card shopping portals and cashback sites. In this chapter, we'll explore how to make the most out of your online purchases by leveraging credit card rewards, exploring cashback options, stacking rewards, and utilizing strategic partnerships.

Using Credit Card Shopping Portals and Cashback Sites

One of the most effective ways to boost your rewards when shopping online is to use credit card shopping portals and cashback websites. These platforms not only provide you with additional saving opportunities but can also amplify the rewards you earn from your credit card. Let's break down how they work.

1. Credit Card Shopping Portals: Many major credit card issuers have their own shopping portals that allow cardholders to earn additional points or cash back for making purchases through affiliated retailers.

a. How They Work

Access the Portal: Start by logging into your credit card account and navigating to the shopping portal. Some popular credit card issuers with shopping portals include Chase Ultimate Rewards, American Express Membership Rewards, and Citi ThankYou.

Browse Retailers: The portal will list various online retailers, often highlighting current promotions. Each retailer typically offers a different rewards rate—generally ranging from 1x to 10x points or a percentage of your purchase as cashback.

Click Through to Shop: After selecting a retailer, click through the link provided in the portal to ensure that your transaction is tracked. This click is essential for earning your bonus rewards.

b. Potential Benefits

Bonus Points or Cash Back: By starting your shopping from the portal, you can earn extra points or cash back on top of what you would earn from your card for the purchase itself.

Special Promotions: Many portals offer limited-time promotions, which can provide even higher rates for certain retailers or categories. Keep an eye on these promotions to maximize earnings.

2. Cashback Sites: Cashback websites function similarly to shopping portals, allowing you to earn a percentage of your purchases back in cash when you shop through their links.

a. How They Work

Join a Cashback Site: Popular cashback sites such as Rakuten (formerly Ebates), TopCashback, and Swagbucks require users to create an account. Registration is typically free, and you can start earning immediately.

Explore Retailers and Offers: Once registered, you can browse the site for various retailers, each offering different cashback percentages. Some retailers may provide additional bonuses for first-time buyers or specific seasonal promotions.

Shop and Claim Cash Back: Similar to shopping portals, you must click through the cashback site's link to the retailer of your choice for your purchase to qualify for cashback. Once your purchase is confirmed, the cashback will accumulate in your account.

b. Potential Benefits

Additional Earnings: Shopping through cashback sites allows you to earn cash back in addition to the rewards offered by your credit card. The cashback can also be significant; some retailers may offer as much as 10% or more on select purchases.

Easy Payout Options: Most cashback sites provide several withdrawal methods, including PayPal, checks, or gift cards, allowing you to choose how you'd like to receive your rewards.

Stack Rewards Through Online Shopping Offers and Partnerships: Maximizing your online shopping rewards isn't just about choosing the right card or cashback site. You can also stack multiple rewards opportunities to enhance your earnings. Here's how.

1. Stacking Multiple Programs

a. Using Both Credit Card Portals and Cashback Sites

Dual Tracking: When shopping online, you can use both your credit card issuer's shopping portal and a cashback site. Depending on the specific policies of these programs, it may be possible to earn rewards from each platform. For example, if you shop through your credit card's portal, you might still qualify for cashback through Rakuten.

Prioritizing Earnings: Check which platform offers a better reward rate before you finalize your purchase. If the cashback percentage on Rakuten is higher than the bonus points offered by your credit card's shopping portal, opt for the cashback site.

b. Aligning Shopping Spree with Promotions

Plan Your Purchases: Align your shopping with promotional events across multiple platforms. For instance, if a cashback site announces a holiday special with doubled rewards at a specific retailer while your credit card portal offers a bonus, schedule your shopping accordingly.

2. Utilize Store-Specific Promotions: Many financial institutions and cashback sites have partnerships with specific stores that may offer additional incentives:

a. Retailer Membership Programs

Extra Points for Loyalty Members: If you frequently shop at a particular store, consider joining its loyalty program. Often, these programs provide bonus points, exclusive discounts, and personalized offers that can be combined with your credit card rewards.

Cross-Promotion Deals: Some retailers offer additional cashback or promotions when using specific credit cards to pay, creating an exciting additional stacking opportunity.

b. Limited Time Offers

Flash Sales and Cash Back Deals: These short-term promotions can significantly increase your rewards potential. For instance, a retailer may run a flash sale offering 20% off everything for 24 hours while also providing 10% cashback through a cashback site.

Social Media Promotions: Stay connected with your favorite retailers on social media for flash sales, coupons, and exclusive rewards opportunities.

3. Refer a Friend Programs: Referral programs increasingly reward both the referrer and the new customer, which can also be utilized tactically to maximize rewards:

Referral Bonuses: Some cashback sites offer referral bonuses when friends sign up through your link. By sharing with friends and family, you can earn a bonus while they benefit from a discount on their first purchase.

4. Earn Points through Payment Method Used: Using payment methods strategically during online shopping can also stack rewards:

Using Store Gift Cards: If you purchase gift cards to your favorite retailers through cashback sites or apps, you can benefit from both cashback and rewards on gift card purchases. Then, when you shop with those gift cards, you can continue to earn rewards through your credit card.

Flexible Payment Options: Some credit cards offer more rewards when certain payment methods are used. If you have a choice between credit card payment or other methods like PayPal, be sure you're using the method that maximizes your rewards.

Maximizing online shopping rewards requires a strategic approach that leverages credit card shopping portals, cashback sites, and promotional offers. By understanding how these platforms work and actively seeking opportunities to stack rewards, you can turn everyday shopping into a lucrative venture.

In this chapter, we covered the importance of selecting the right credit cards, utilizing cashback sites, and taking advantage of limited-time deals and partnerships to amplify your earnings. With the right tactics in place, you can transform your online shopping habits into a reward-generating powerhouse, putting you in a position to earn significant cashback or points on purchases you were planning to make anyway.

You'll be well-equipped to make informed spending decisions that maximize your rewards potential across various sectors, ultimately enriching your financial well-being and lifestyle.

$$$$$$$$$

Chapter 13

Taking Advantage of Referral Bonuses

One of the lesser-known yet highly effective strategies for maximizing rewards in your financial plan lies in leveraging referral bonuses. Many credit card issuers and loyalty programs offer enticing referral incentives that allow users to earn extra points or cash back for bringing new customers into their fold. By sharing the perks of your favorite card or program with friends and family, you not only help them potentially land a valuable product but also unlock various bonuses for yourself.

In this chapter, we will explore how you can earn extra points by referring friends and family, understand the limits and structures of these referral bonuses, and strategize effectively to maximize your earnings.

Earning Extra Points by Referring Friends and Family

1. The Power of Word-of-Mouth Marketing: In an age where personal recommendations carry significant weight, credit card companies have tapped into this concept by creating referral programs that reward existing customers for promoting their offerings. When you refer a friend or family member to apply for a specific credit card or join a loyalty program, you often earn substantial bonuses if they successfully sign up and meet certain conditions.

2. How Referral Programs Work: Most credit card companies have streamlined the referral process, making it easy for users to share their experiences and benefits with others. Here's how it typically works:

a. Finding Your Referral Link

Accessing the Program: Log into your credit card account on the issuer's website or app. Many card issuers prominently display referral programs on their dashboards or within the rewards section.

Customized Referral Links: Once you locate the referral program, you will usually be provided with a unique referral link. This personalized link tracks your referrals, ensuring that you receive the appropriate bonuses if someone uses it to apply for the card.

b. Spreading the Word

Digital Sharing Options: Most credit card issuers make it easy to share your referral link through email, social media, or text. Take advantage of these platforms to reach a broadened audience.

Personalized Recommendations: Instead of just sending the link, share your positive experiences with the credit card, including details about benefits, rewards, and any promotions that may entice others.

3. Types of Referral Bonuses: The bonuses you can earn through referral programs vary by credit card issuer and can include:

a. Points or Miles Bonuses

Tiered Points Structures: Many credit card issuers offer a fixed number of points for each successful referral. For example, you might earn 10,000 points for each new cardholder who signs up and meets the minimum spending requirement.

Limited-Time Promotions: Occasionally, issuers run promotion cycles in which the points earned for referrals are boosted—potentially offering double or triple the usual amount for a short time.

b. Cashback Offers

Direct Cash Bonuses: Some cards provide cash rewards instead of points. This could be something like $100 for each successful referral, directly deposited into your account after the new customer meets specific requirements.

Reward Multipliers: Even for cards primarily focused on earning points, some offers may include a tangible cash bonus for referring individuals who sign up.

4. Maximizing Your Referrals: To make the most of these referral opportunities, consider the following strategies:

a. Targeted Sharing

Identify Potential Referrals: Think about friends, family, or colleagues who might benefit from your credit card. Are there specific individuals with spending habits that align well with your card's rewards structure? A strategic approach can lead to higher success rates.

b. Timing is Key

Make the Most of Promotions: Keep an eye on your issuer's referral page for any seasonal promotions that heighten referral bonuses. Timing your outreach during these events can significantly enhance your earning potential.

c. Educate Your Referrals

Customization for Potential Refs: Give your referrals information about why you use the card, emphasizing specific benefits like high rewards rates for groceries, dining, or travel. Offering insights into your actual experiences can help sway their decision.

Understanding Referral Limits and Bonus Structures: While referral bonuses present an excellent opportunity to accumulate rewards, it's equally important to comprehend the limitations and structures that accompany these programs.

1. Referral Limits

a. Annual Limits

Know the Cap: Most credit card issuers impose a cap on the number of referral bonuses you can earn in a given year. This could range from a few to several dozen successful referrals, depending on the card and the issuer's policy.

Check Your Card's Terms: Always refer to the specific terms and conditions of your card's referral program to fully understand your limits.

This is crucial to ensuring you don't miss out on potential rewards.

b. Tiered Bonuses

Graduated Scaling: Some programs offer tiered structures where the bonus increases after you reach certain thresholds. For example, you might earn $50 per referral for the first five and $75 for any subsequent referrals within the same promotion cycle.

c. Inactivity Clauses

Stale Referrals: If a referral doesn't sign up within a specified timeframe (generally ranging from 30 to 90 days), you might lose your chance to earn that bonus. Make sure your referrals understand any deadlines they need to meet.

2. Bonus Structures

a. Minimum Spending Requirements

Know the Spending Conditions: In many cases, while you might successfully refer a friend, you won't earn your bonus unless they meet certain spending thresholds within the first few months of account opening. Typically, this might involve a requirement to spend a certain amount within 3 months of being approved for the card.

b. Credit Approval Dependency

Eligibility: Referral bonuses typically only apply when a new cardholder is approved for the credit card. If your referred friend doesn't meet credit criteria, you won't receive your bonus.

3. Keeping It Ethical

a. Honesty in Recommendations

Transparency: While it's tempting to push the benefits of your card aggressively, it's essential to maintain ethical standards in your referral practices. Be upfront about the card's terms, including any fees or potential downsides.

b. Avoiding Spam

Quality Over Quantity: Rather than bombarding people with referral links indiscriminately, aim to refer individuals who would genuinely benefit from the card. This ethical approach can help maintain your relationships and build trust.

Taking advantage of referral bonuses provides a fantastic opportunity to boost your credit card rewards significantly. By strategically referring friends and family, you position yourself to earn extra points or cashback while helping loved ones discover valuable financial products.

Understanding how referral programs work, setting realistic expectations concerning limits, and navigating the bonus structures can significantly enhance your earning potential. With proper planning and ethical engagement, you can turn your enthusiasm for your credit cards into tangible rewards that enrich your financial journey.

As we conclude this chapter, it is essential to remain informed about the ongoing changes in credit card initiatives and adapt to new referral programs as they emerge. Moving forward, we will delve into specialized areas of managing your finances effectively, including travel rewards and redeeming points, ensuring you can maximize every dollar spent to its fullest potential.

Chapter 14
Credit Card Reward Multipliers and Special Deals

In an increasingly competitive credit card market, issuers are constantly striving to attract new customers and retain existing ones by offering appealing rewards programs. One of the most enticing features is the concept of reward multipliers, which allow cardholders to earn more points, miles, or cash back on specific categories of purchases. Understanding how to select cards with higher multipliers for frequent purchases and leveraging seasonal promotional deals can significantly enhance your rewards earnings.

In this chapter, we will explore strategies for finding lucrative reward multipliers and provide tips for maximizing the benefit of seasonal and promotional rewards.

Finding Cards with Higher Multipliers for Frequent Purchases

1. Understanding Reward Multipliers: Reward multipliers are mechanisms by which credit card issuers incentivize spending in particular categories. Typically expressed in a format such as "3x points" or "5% cash back," these multipliers allow consumers to accumulate rewards faster based on their buying habits.

a. Categories of Rewards

Grocery Stores: Many cards offer higher multipliers for spending at grocery stores, capitalizing on the fact that groceries are a necessary and regular expenditure. This can range from 2x to even 6x points or cash back, depending on the card.

Dining and Restaurants: Cards focused on dining rewards often provide 2x to 5x multipliers for restaurant purchases. If you dine out frequently, a card tailored for restaurant spending can yield significant returns.

Travel and Gas: For frequent travelers or commuters, cards with elevated rewards for gas stations or travel-related purchases can amplify your earnings while covering essential expenses.

Online Shopping: Many cards now cater to the growing trend of e-commerce with higher rewards for online purchases. This can be particularly valuable during sales seasons, when you may be buying more than usual.

2. Researching Quality Cards: Not all credit cards are created equal, and finding the ones that best suit your spending habits is crucial. Here's how to do it effectively:

a. Card Comparisons

Utilize Comparison Tools: Numerous websites allow consumers to compare credit cards based on reward structures, fees, and benefits. Utilize these tools to find cards that align with your spending in specific categories. Websites like NerdWallet, Credit Karma, and The Points Guy provide updated and comprehensive comparisons.

Look for Sign-Up Bonuses: Many cards offer significant point bonuses if you meet a minimum spending threshold within the initial months of account opening. This can amplify the rewards you can earn from the start.

b. Read the Fine Print

Understand Eligibility and Limits: Make sure to read the terms and conditions associated with the card, especially regarding reward multipliers. Look for potential limits on how many transactions can qualify under the multipliers within a billing cycle and any necessary conditions.

Check for Rotating Categories: Some cards, such as those in the Discover and Chase Freedom line, rotate their bonus categories each quarter. While these cards can offer higher rewards in certain categories, it's beneficial to remember when the categories shift to maximize your earnings.

3. Aligning Cards with Spending Habits: To effectively optimize your rewards, you should align your credit card use with your spending habits:

a. Analyze Your Monthly Expenses

Track Your Spending: Review your monthly expenses to identify where you are spending the most. Take notes on your expenditures to see if you regularly shop at places that offer higher multipliers.

Select Cards Accordingly: For example, if you find that groceries make up a significant portion of your spending, consider acquiring a card with elevated rewards for grocery purchases.

b. Card Stacking

Utilize Multiple Cards: If you frequently spend in diverse categories, consider applying for multiple cards designed to maximize rewards across different types of spending. This may include a card with strong grocery rewards and another that excels in dining or travel.

Combine Rewards: Some issuers allow you to combine points earned across several cards into one account, making it easier to redeem them for travel, merchandise, or cash back.

Tips for Seasonal and Promotional Rewards Multipliers: Seasonal trends and promotional events present perfect opportunities to capitalize on bonus rewards. Understanding how to strategically utilize these can significantly elevate your rewards-earning potential.

1. Taking Advantage of Seasonal Promotions

a. Identify Key Shopping Seasons

Holidays and Events: Key shopping periods such as the holiday season, Black Friday, Cyber Monday, and back-to-school sales often come with additional promotional multipliers by credit card issuers. During these times, many cards offer boosted points or cash back percentages for spending in specific categories.

End of Year Spending: Look for promotions during the end-of-year shopping spree. Issuers may provide temporary increases in rewards rates to encourage card use.

b. Sign Up for Notifications

Stay in the Loop: Subscribe to newsletters from your credit card issuer. Many issuers send out alerts about current promotions, including limited-time offers that can enhance your multipliers or bonus rewards.

Social Media Engagement: Follow your issuer on social media for updates on exclusive offers or flash sales. Some issuers promote unique seasonal bonuses or special multiplier events solely through their social channels.

2. Leveraging Promotional Offers

a. Bonus Point Events

Special Promotions: Occasionally, issuers will feature flash promotions offering bonus points for specific categories or retailers for a limited time. Look for these notifications, especially around key shopping events.

Targeted Offers: Credit card companies offer personalized discounts to cardholders based on their spending patterns. Check your account regularly for these targeted promotions that may provide additional multipliers for stores or services you frequently use.

b. Holiday-Specific Multiplier Categories

Holiday Shopping Bonuses: Many credit cards provide special multipliers for retail purchases during significant holidays. For instance, a card might offer 5x points for all purchases made in December or limited-time bonuses for certain retailers around the holidays.

Seasonal Travel Offers: For travel enthusiasts, look out for seasonal promotions that may offer higher rewards multipliers for hotel stays, flights, or car rentals during peak seasons, ensuring you take advantage when you're likely to spend.

3. Planning Purchases Around Promotions

a. Sync Purchases with Offers

Plan Ahead: If you know you'll be making significant purchases, like buying gifts or planning a vacation, plan to use your cards during promotional periods to take advantage of higher multipliers.

Budgeting: Consider altering your typical purchasing habits based on seasonal multipliers. This could involve delaying a purchase until a promotional event or shifting spending categories to maximize your bonus points.

b. Use Cashback and Discount Promotions Together

Stack Offers: During promotional periods, try to combine cashback offers from your credit card with additional discounts from retailers. This could be a special cashback event from your card alongside a retail partner sale.

Use Those Referral Benefits: If you've previously earned benefits from referrals, use those bonuses wisely. For peak shopping seasons or events, any additional points or cashback received can be used strategically to enhance your rewards further.

Understanding and leveraging credit card reward multipliers and special deals is essential for any savvy consumer looking to maximize rewards. By selecting cards that offer higher multipliers aligned with your spending habits and taking advantage of seasonal promotions, you can significantly enhance your earnings.

Researching your options, tracking your expenses, and strategically timing your purchases around promotional events will not only increase the points or cash back you earn, but also ensure you are getting the most value out of your everyday spending.

As you move forward with your financial journey, remember to stay informed about changing rewards programs, periodic promotions, and emerging credit card offers that can help amplify your earnings.

$$$$$$$$$

Chapter 15

Understanding Annual Fees and Justifying Their Cost

As you navigate the world of credit cards, one topic that frequently arises is the annual fee. For many cardholders, these fees can provoke a sense of hesitation or skepticism, why should you pay a fee annually just for having a credit card? However, what may initially seem like a financial burden can, in fact, represent a pathway to enhanced benefits, greater rewards, and overall financial success.

In this chapter, we will explore how to evaluate whether an annual fee is worth it, as well as discuss effective strategies to use perks and rewards to offset that cost.

Understanding Annual Fees

1. What Are Annual Fees? An annual fee is a charge that credit card issuers apply for the convenience of using their card and accessing its associated benefits. This fee typically ranges from $20 to several hundred dollars, depending on the card's features, target market, and rewards structure. Some cards come with no annual fee, while others offer extensive benefits that can make the cost worthwhile.

2. Types of Credit Cards with Annual Fees

Premium Rewards Cards: These may offer extensive rewards on travel, dining, cash back, or other categories, along with perks like airport lounge access, travel insurance, and concierge services.

Cash Back and Store-Specific Cards: Some cards in these categories have lower annual fees and often provide bonuses for specific purchases, making them appealing for regular spending.

Business Credit Cards: Business cards generally have annual fees that correspond to the various perks designed to meet the needs of business owners, such as expense tracking and higher rewards on office supplies.

Evaluating If an Annual Fee Is Worth It

1. Analyzing Your Spending Habits: To determine whether an annual fee is justified, it's essential to assess your individual spending patterns:

a. Categorize Your Expenses

Identify Core Spending Areas: Make a list detailing your monthly expenditures, identifying which categories you spend the most on. This can include groceries, dining, travel, entertainment, and recurring bills.

Calculate Potential Rewards: Consider how a rewards card with an annual fee might yield greater rewards in these categories compared to a no-fee card. If the fees allow you to accumulate points or cash back significantly faster in your primary spending areas, it could warrant the cost.

2. Comparing Rewards and Perks

a. Value of Earned Rewards

Point and Cash Back Values: Investigate the points structure of cards with annual fees. For instance, if a card offers 3x points on travel and your monthly travel expenses total $500, you're potentially earning 1,500 points monthly. Over a year, that could translate to substantial rewards that far exceed the fee.

Evaluate Redemption Options: Consider how you can redeem those points. If the issuer has advantageous redemption policies, such as cashback or travel perks, it can increase the effective value of your rewards tremendously.

b. Assessing Perks and Benefits

Travel Benefits: If you frequently travel, look for features such as airline fee reimbursements, hotel discounts, or global entry/tSA Precheck credits that might effectively reduce your travel costs, thereby justifying the annual fee.

Insurance Coverage: Some credit cards include travel insurance, purchase protection, and extended warranties, which can save you substantial money in the long run. Assess whether these features contribute to the overall value of the card compared to the annual fee.

3. Using Future Spending Projections

a. Life Changes Impacting Spending

Anticipate Changes: Assess how your spending habits may change in the years to come. If you anticipate increased expenditures in the areas targeted by a particular card (e.g., birth of a child, new job requiring travel), calculate how that might affect the perceived value of the card's rewards versus its fees.

b. Researching Card Offers Over Time

Promotional Deals: Card issuers regularly update their offers and rewards structures. Stay informed about promotions that may allow you to benefit further from the card without an adjustment to your annual fee or through opportunities like bonus points if you meet specific spending minimums.

Using Perks and Rewards to Offset the Fee

1. Maximizing Card Benefits: To make an annual fee worthwhile, you need to actively engage with and take full advantage of the benefits offered by your credit card.

a. Loyalty Programs Integration

Align with Airlines and Hotels: If your card offers bonuses for spending with specific airlines or hotel chains, make it a point to book travel through those partners. This punctuality can accumulate points more quickly and yield higher rewards, effectively offsetting the annual fee.

Stacking Rewards: Pair your credit card with loyalty programs (e.g., frequent flyer miles, hotel loyalty points) to magnify your earnings. The synergy between these rewards can lead to compensatory benefits that far exceed the card's annual fee.

2. Making Use of Statement Credits and Other Offers

a. Leveraging Statement Credits

Targeted Offers: Some cards offer statement credits for particular purchases, such as subscription services or dining. These offer additional savings and effectively reduce the upfront cost represented by the annual fee.

Annual Fee Credits: Certain premium cards come with a feature that reimburses part or all of the annual fee if you spend a particular amount on the card outside of any targeted categories.

b. Utilizing Travel Perks

Airport Lounge Access: If your card provides complimentary access to airport lounges, calculate the amount you would typically spend on food and beverages in airports. This benefit alone can offset the annual fee if you travel frequently.

Free Checked Bags and Priority Boarding: Calculate how much you typically spend on checked bags and boarding upgrades. If your card provides these services at no additional cost for cardholders, the savings can quickly justify the annual cost.

3. Tracking and Documenting Savings
a. Maintain a Rewards Log

Record Card Use: Keep a log of how much you earn through the card on a monthly and annual basis. Include additional aspects, such as saved money through perks, travel benefits, and other rewards.

Measure Against Annual Fees: Create a simple formula comparing the annual fee against your calculated savings from the card. This can provide a visual and quantitative sense of whether the fee is genuinely justifiable based on accumulated benefits.

b. Annual Review Process

Conduct a Yearly Review: Set aside time each year to review your credit card offers, spending, and gained rewards. Make adjustments as necessary, switching to cards that may better cater to your current lifestyle and spending habits.

Understanding and justifying annual fees on credit cards requires an objective assessment of your financial habits, spending patterns, and how best to leverage available perks and rewards. While it may initially appear daunting, winning the battle against annual fees involves a deep dive into the value offered versus the cost.

By thoughtfully analyzing your spending, strategically utilizing card benefits, and regularly reviewing your financial decisions, you can make educated choices that not only justify annual fees but turn them into a substantial advantage in your overall financial strategy.

$$$$$$$$$

Chapter 16

Avoiding Common Pitfalls to Maximize Rewards

In the pursuit of maximizing credit card rewards, it's not enough to simply choose the right cards; you also must navigate the landscape carefully to avoid common pitfalls that can negate the benefits of those rewards. Interest charges, fees, and missed payments can quickly erode the value of any rewards you earn, transforming what should be a positive financial tool into a burden. In this chapter, we will explore essential tips for avoiding interest and fees, as well as strategies for managing payments effectively to safeguard your rewards journey.

Tips for Avoiding Interest and Fees That Can Negate Rewards

1. Understanding Interest Rates

a. Annual Percentage Rate (APR): The Annual Percentage Rate (APR) is the interest rate applied to your unpaid balance. Knowing your card's APR is critical because if you carry a balance from one month to the next, the interest charged can quickly negate the rewards you've earned.

b. How Interest Accrues: Interest on most credit cards is calculated daily based on your average daily balance. Thus, the longer you carry a balance, the more interest you'll accrue. To avoid high-interest costs, aim to pay off your balance in full each month.

2. Paying Attention to Fees

a. Understanding Fees: There are various fees associated with credit cards that can chip away at your rewards:

Annual Fees: Although many premium cards charge these fees, it's essential to ensure that the rewards and perks you receive justify the cost.

Late Payment Fees: Missing a payment can result in hefty late fees, which can vary widely by issuer but typically range from $25 to $39.

Foreign Transaction Fees: If your travel plans include foreign countries, be wary of cards that charge fees for transactions made outside of the home country, usually around 1%-3% of each transaction.

Balance Transfer and Cash Advance Fees: These fees can add an extra layer of cost if you access
funds through a cash advance or transfer balances from another card.

b. Choosing the Right Card to Avoid Fees: When selecting a credit card, look for those that have minimal or no fees for foreign transactions, balance transfers, or cash advances. Additionally, weigh the benefits of premium cards with annual fees against the potential rewards you might earn.

How to Manage Payments to Avoid Penalties?

1. Setting Up Automatic Payments

a. Ensuring Timely Payments: Setting up automatic payments is one of the most effective ways to ensure you never miss a due date. This approach can substantially reduce the risk of incurring late fees and help keep your account in good standing.

Minimum Payment Option: Designate an automatic payment for at least the minimum due each month. This will avoid late fees and keep your account compliant, but it's best to pay the full balance whenever possible to prevent interest from accumulating.

Full Payment Option: If your cash flow allows, consider setting up your automatic payments to pay your balance in full. This strategy prevents interest from accruing and maximizes the rewards value.

2. Utilizing Alerts and Reminders

a. Setting Up Alerts: Take advantage of technology by utilizing your card issuer's mobile app or online banking portal to set up alerts.

Notifications can remind you of upcoming due dates, spending limits, and even provide an overview of current balances.

Due Date Alerts: Receive alerts a few days before your payment is due to ensure you have ample time to prepare the funds.

Spending Alerts: Monitor your spending with alerts for when you approach a specific dollar amount. This can prevent you from overspending and ensure you're able to pay off your balance in full.

3. Keeping Track of Your Credit Card Usage

a. Regularly Reviewing Statements: Make it a habit to review your credit card statements, either through email alerts or by logging into your account regularly. This will help you catch any discrepancies, unauthorized transactions, or unexpected fees early.

Monthly Budgeting: Create a monthly budget that includes your credit card usage to help you manage spending effectively and ensure you have the funds available to pay off your balance.

b. Using Financial Apps: Consider leveraging financial management apps that allow you to track your spending across all your accounts, including credit cards. These tools can centralize your finances and provide insights into your spending habits.

4. Understanding Grace Periods

a. What is a Grace Period? Many credit cards offer a grace period, which is typically 21 to 25 days after the end of a billing cycle where you can pay your balance in full without incurring interest charges.

Populating Your Knowledge: Ensure you fully understand your card's grace period policies. If you pay your balance before this period ends, you won't face interest charges, thus maximizing your rewards earning potential.

b. Using the Grace Period Wisely: To make the most of your grace period, consider timing your purchases effectively close to the end of your billing cycle. This enables you to take advantage of the grace period without incurring interest charges, allowing you to maximize your credit the following month.

5. Strategies for Boosting Your Cash Flow

a. Establishing an Emergency Fund: Having an emergency fund can protect your credit card from unexpected expenses that could lead to high balances and missed payments. Aim for at least three to six months' worth of living expenses in a separate, accessible savings account.

b. Budgeting for Rewards: If your primary goal is to maximize rewards, consider adjusting your overall budget to prioritize spending in categories that earn you the most points or cash back. For example, ensure that necessary monthly expenses align with the benefits offered by your cards, rather than spending from random impulse purchases.

Maximizing rewards from credit cards requires not only choosing the right cards but also navigating your credit use wisely. By proactively managing payments, avoiding fees, and avoiding interest, you can ensure that the rewards you earn don't get overshadowed by costly mistakes.

By paying attention to interest rates and fees, setting up automated payments, utilizing alerts, and understanding grace periods, you create a robust strategy to safeguard your financial future while earning the maximum possible rewards.

Delve into the intricacies of redeeming rewards, learning how to make the most of what you have earned through careful credit card use. Explore best practices for leveraging your points, miles, and cash back for maximum value, ensuring your efforts in earning rewards result in tangible benefits.

$$$$$$$$$

Chapter 17
Building and Protecting Your Credit Score

Your credit score is a critical aspect of your financial health, influencing your ability to secure loans, qualify for favorable interest rates, and impact other financial opportunities such as renting an apartment or getting car insurance. Therefore, understanding how responsible credit card use can improve your credit score and knowing how to protect that score while maximizing rewards are essential to your financial well-being.

In this chapter, we will explore the mechanics of credit scores, how credit cards impact these scores, and effective strategies for protecting your credit while enjoying the rewards your card offers.

Understanding How Responsible Credit Card Use Builds Credit

1. The Basics of Credit Scores: Credit scores typically range from 300 to 850 and are calculated based on various factors:

Payment History (35%): This is the most significant factor. It reflects your history of making payments on time. Late payments, defaults, and bankruptcies can severely impact your score.

Credit Utilization (30%): Credit utilization measures how much credit you're using compared to your total credit limit. A lower utilization ratio is favorable.

Length of Credit History (15%): This considers how long your accounts have been active. Generally, the longer your credit history, the better it is for your score.

Types of Credit (10%): A mix of credit accounts, such as credit cards, mortgages, and installment loans, can benefit your score.

Recent Inquiries (10%): When you apply for new credit, lenders perform hard inquiries that slightly impact your score.

2. How Credit Cards Influence Your Credit Score: Credit cards are powerful tools that can help
you build a solid credit history when used responsibly.

a. Establishing a Payment History: By consistently paying your credit card bill on time, you develop a positive payment history, which is a significant factor in your credit score. Setting up automatic payments or reminders can help you stay on track.

b. Managing Credit Utilization: Your credit utilization ratio is calculated by dividing your total credit card balances by your total credit limits. A rule of thumb is to keep your utilization below 30%, though many experts recommend aiming for below 10% for optimal scoring.

Example: If you have a combined limit of $10,000 across all your cards and your total balance is $1,500, your credit utilization ratio is 15%.

c. Length of Credit History and New Accounts: Opening new credit accounts can affect your average account age, but responsible use of new cards can contribute positively in the long run. If you maintain your old accounts, especially those with positive payment histories, they contribute to lengthening your credit history.

d. Diversity of Credit Types: Having a mix of credit types can enhance your score. If you've only used credit cards, consider responsibly taking on a different type of debt, like a small personal loan, to diversify your credit profile.

3. Understanding the Impact of Hard Inquiries: When you apply for new credit, lenders perform hard inquiries, which can temporarily lower your score. Limit applications for new credit and time them carefully to mitigate the impact.

Tip: If you are considering several credit card applications, try to do so within a short timeframe (like 30 days). Many scoring models will count multiple inquiries for the same type of credit as one inquiry if done in that period.

Tips for Protecting Your Score While Maximizing Rewards

1. Stay Within Your Budget

a. Keep Track of Spending: As you aim to earn rewards, ensure your spending doesn't exceed your means. Create a budget that includes your credit card expenses and stick to it to avoid overspending and carrying a balance.

b. Use Credit Cards for Essential Purchases: Focus on using your credit card for planned purchases where you can afford to pay off the balance in full each month. This practice will earn you rewards while avoiding interest accrual that can damage your score.

2. Regularly Monitor Your Credit

a. Obtain Free Credit Reports: In the United States, you're entitled to one free credit report from each of the three major credit bureaus (Experian, TransUnion, and Equifax) every year. Use AnnualCreditReport.com to access these reports.

b. Credit Monitoring Services: Consider subscribing to credit monitoring services that alert you of changes in your credit report, including new accounts or missed payments. Many banks and credit card issuers offer free monitoring services that can help you stay informed.

3. Maintain a Healthy Credit Utilization Ratio

a. Spread Your Spending Across Cards: If you have multiple credit cards, consider spreading your purchases across them rather than maxing out one card. This approach helps maintain a lower credit utilization ratio.

b. Consider Requesting a Credit Limit Increase: If your financial situation allows for it, requesting an increase in your credit limit can help lower your utilization ratio when balances remain the same. This should be done responsibly, and you should avoid increasing your spending as a result.

4. Pay Your Bills on Time

a. Use Automatic Billing: Set up automatic payments or reminders to ensure you meet all due dates. Even one missed payment can negatively affect your credit score and your ability to earn rewards.

b. Split Payments: If your budget is tight in a particular month, consider splitting your payments into two or more smaller payments to spread your expenses throughout the month. This can help avoid carrying a large balance that could affect your utilization ratio.

5. Re-evaluate Your Credit Card Portfolio

a. Assess Annual Fees vs. Rewards: Periodically review your credit cards to ensure that the rewards and perks justify their costs. If a card incurs fees that outweigh the benefits, consider downgrading or closing the account. However, closing accounts can negatively affect your credit score if it reduces your overall credit limit or length of credit history.

b. Target Cards that Enhance Your Credit Profile: Look for credit cards that have features beneficial to your credit score—such as those with higher limits, lower interest rates, or certain benefits like cash back or travel rewards that suit your spending habits.

6. Be Cautious with New Applications

a. Limit Hard Inquiries: Be selective about the new credit accounts you open to avoid multiple hard inquiries, which can detrimentally affect your credit score. Research cards thoroughly to find the best fit before applying.

b. Timing Matters: Timing your credit applications is crucial. If planning to make a significant financial decision, such as buying a home, avoid opening new accounts at least a few months in advance to give your score time to recover from any inquiries.

Building and protecting your credit score requires a combination of strategic credit card use, knowledge, and diligence. By understanding how responsible credit card habits influence your credit score, you can effectively elevate your score while earning rewards.

Utilizing budgeting techniques, regularly monitoring your credit, maintaining a healthy utilization ratio, ensuring timely payment of bills, and being thoughtful about your credit card portfolio will help you protect your credit score. This strategy not only enhances your purchasing power but also positions you for better financial opportunities in the future.

From travel perks to cash back options, mastering the art of redemption is key to optimizing your overall credit card rewards journey, making it all the more rewarding and beneficial to your financial lifestyle.

$$$$$$$$$

Chapter 18

Advanced Redemption Techniques

As you progress through your credit card rewards journey, understanding how to effectively redeem your points for maximum value is crucial. The vast array of redemption options can often lead to confusion, particularly when navigating different programs and their respective value propositions.

In this chapter, we will delve into advanced techniques for redeeming points, focusing on strategies for getting the highest value—such as first-class travel and luxury hotel stays—while also highlighting ways to avoid low-value redemptions.

Tips for Redeeming Points for the Highest Value

1. Understanding Value per Point

a. Calculating Value: Before redeeming your points, it's essential to understand what each point or mile is worth. The value can vary significantly based on how you choose to redeem them. For instance, travel rewards often yield a higher redemption value than cash back or gift cards.

Example: If you have a travel reward of 50,000 points that can be used for a $500 flight, the value of each point would be calculated. On the other hand, if you find a flight that costs $1,000 for the same number of points, your value per point would be also calculated accordingly. This demonstrates why finding the right redemption option is crucial.

b. Researching Transfer Partners: Many travel rewards programs allow you to transfer points to various airline and hotel partners. This transfer can dramatically increase the value of your points.

Airline Partners: For example, if you're a member of a flexible rewards program like Chase Ultimate Rewards, you can transfer your points to partners like United Airlines or British Airways for higher value redemptions, especially for premium cabin awards.

Hotel Partners: Some hotel loyalty programs allow you to redeem points for expensive nights at luxury hotels at a fraction of the price. Look into the program terms to see how points can be used for premium experiences.

2. Booking First-Class Travel: First-class flights offer one of the highest values for point redemptions, particularly on international routes. Here's how to leverage your points effectively for first-class experiences:

a. Utilizing Airline Alliances: Many airlines are part of global alliances such as Star Alliance or

Oneworld. Booking first-class tickets through these alliances can yield substantial savings in points.

Example: If you have points through one airline but want to fly with another airline's first-class service, check if your points can be transferred to the airline in the same alliance, often allowing you to book luxurious routes at reduced point costs.

b. Finding Award Availability: Airlines often release a limited number of seats for award travel, especially in premium classes. Advanced planning and flexibility regarding dates can improve your chances of finding first-class seats.

Tools: Utilize tools like Google Flights or airline-specific search engines to determine which flights have award availability. Keep in mind that booking at least 6-12 months in advance will usually yield the best options.

c. Consider Using Points for Upgrades: Instead of burning a large number of points for a first-class ticket, consider using them to upgrade from an economy fare. This option can often represent better value, especially if you secure a low-cost economy ticket.

3. Taking Advantage of Luxury Hotels: Redeeming points for luxury hotel stays can provide unforgettable experiences at a lower cost. Here are tips for maximizing value when booking luxury accommodations:

a. Point Breaks and Promotions: Many hotel loyalty programs frequently run promotions or "Point Breaks" offers, allowing you to book luxury hotels for a fraction of the usual points required.

Example: Marriott Bonvoy and IHG Rewards Club often feature reduced-point nights at luxury properties. Subscribe to alerts to stay up-to-date on these promotions.

b. Searching for Unique Experiences: Some hotel reward programs offer unique experiences (like private dinners, spa treatments, and exclusive tours)

as redemption options. These can sometimes represent higher value than traditional cash bookings.

c. Leveraging Points for Premium Experiences: If you're looking to experience a high-end hotel, go beyond simply booking a room. Consider redeeming points for experiences curated by those properties, such as a luxury spa day or an exclusive culinary experience.

4. Timing Your Redemptions

a. Off-Peak Travel: It's often easier and cheaper to redeem points for flights and hotel stays during off-peak seasons. Evaluate the travel calendar of your preferred airlines and hotels to identify when award availability and lower-point redemptions are most accessible.

b. Last-Minute Redemptions: While often considered risky, last-minute travel redemptions can sometimes yield sensational values, particularly if airlines or hotels aim to fill unsold capacity. Just be sure to have flexible plans.

How to Avoid Low-Value Redemptions?

1. Understanding Low-Value Redemptions: Low-value redemptions are often those that convert points to merchandise, cash back, or gift cards at a significantly reduced value. If you're receiving just 0.5 cents per point, you've probably fallen into a low-value redemption trap.

2. Avoiding Merchandise Redemption: Redeeming points for electronics, household items, or gift cards might seem tempting but often results in poor value. In many cases, retailers offer sales that reduce these items' price below what you'd pay in points.

Tip: Before opting for merchandise redemption, calculate the value of the item in terms of points and compare it to booking options for travel or hotel stays.

3. Cash Back Options: While cash back might seem an easy win, it usually provides a much lower value than travel redemptions. For instance, a credit card that offers 1% cash back would effectively translate to a mere point value of less than 1 cent.

Recommendation: Focus on redeeming travel rewards over cash back, which will generally yield higher returns in value.

4. Monitoring Your Point Portfolio

a. Stay Informed on Expiration Policies: Some points expire after a certain period of inactivity. Regularly engage with your rewards programs to keep your points active. Travel with different partners, refer a friend, or keep an eye on your point balances to prevent them from expiring unexpectedly.

b. Consolidating Points in Flexible Programs: If you have points across multiple rewards programs, consider consolidating your points into a single, flexible program where you can transfer them to various partners. This consolidation usually maximizes your redemption options and potential value.

5. Avoid Impulsive Decisions: High-value redemptions often require patience and research. Avoid the temptation to redeem points without evaluating the options. Rushing into a low-value redemption can diminish your overall rewards experience.

Mastering advanced redemption techniques is a vital skill in maximizing the value of your hard-earned points. By understanding the nuances of calculating point values, exploring first-class travel and luxury accommodations, timing your redemptions, and avoiding low-value options, you can elevate your travel and experiences to new heights.

The rewards landscape can be complex, but with careful planning and strategic thinking, you can turn your points into extraordinary travel adventures and luxurious stays rather than settling for low-value redemptions.

Whether it's future travels or financial opportunities, being equipped with the right knowledge can make all the difference in your rewards experience.

$$$$$$$$$

Chapter 19
Leveraging Cardholder Benefits Beyond Rewards

While maximizing rewards through strategic spending and redemption is critical to getting the most from your credit cards, many consumers overlook the plethora of cardholder benefits that can greatly enhance their overall experience. From purchase protection and extended warranties to travel insurance and concierge services, these benefits often add significant value to your credit card use, making it an even more advantageous tool in your financial arsenal.

In this chapter, we'll explore these cardholder benefits in detail and provide insights into how you can leverage them effectively to save money, enhance your lifestyle, and protect your purchases.

Understanding Cardholder Benefits: Credit cards today offer a variety of perks beyond just points and cash back. The benefits can vary significantly based on the card issuer and the specific card type (e.g., premium versus basic cards). Knowing what benefits your card provides is crucial to making the most of them.

1. Purchase Protection

a. What is Purchase Protection? Purchase protection is a benefit that typically covers new purchases against theft, damage, or loss within a specified period (usually 90 to 120 days) after the purchase is made. This benefit is often available on many credit cards, especially those geared towards consumers who make significant purchases.

b. How to Leverage Purchase Protection

Document Your Purchases: Keep the receipt and any documentation, including the card statement, as proof of purchase. This is essential for filing a claim.

Filing a Claim: If an item is damaged or stolen, you can file a purchase protection claim through your card issuer. Many issuers have straightforward online systems for managing claims.

Be sure to submit your claim within the required period.

Keep an Eye on Qualifying Criteria: Understand the terms and conditions around the benefit. Some exclusions apply—for example, items lost in transit or damage due to typical wear and tear may not qualify.

2. Extended Warranties

a. What is an Extended Warranty? Many credit cards automatically extend the manufacturer's warranty on newly purchased items, often doubling the length of the coverage (typically for an additional year). This is particularly valuable for electronics, appliances, and more.

b. Making the Most of Extended Warranties

Eligible Items: Check which types of purchases are eligible for coverage. Generally, new consumer goods qualify, but it's essential to review the terms.

Keep Your Receipts: Just like purchase protection, retaining your receipts and warranty documents is crucial for filing a claim. Make sure to register your product if required.

Claim Process: Familiarize yourself with the steps required to initiate a warranty claim. If you have a malfunctioning item that has broken down within the warranty period, gather your receipts, original warranty documentation, and follow your card issuer's claim submission guidelines.

3. Price Matching

a. What is Price Matching? Some credit cards offer price matching benefits, which allow you to receive a refund of the price difference if you find a lower price for a purchased item shortly after buying it.

b. How to Use Price Matching Benefits

Research Post-Purchase: After buying an item, it's beneficial to check prices at other retailers frequently. This will maximize your chances of finding a lower price within the stipulated timeframe (often 30 days).

Submit Your Methodology: When you find a lower price, gather the evidence, including receipts, advertisements, or online listings. Each card issuer has different procedures for submitting these claims, so ensure you're following the correct process.

Understand the Terms: Some price match guarantees may have specific conditions like applicable stores or types of items, so make sure to read the guidelines thoroughly.

Leveraging Insurance Benefits

4. Rental Car Insurance

a. What is Rental Car Insurance? Many credit cards come with rental car insurance that covers damage to or theft of a rental vehicle. This coverage often acts as primary insurance, which can relieve you from having to purchase extra insurance directly from the rental company.

b. Using Rental Car Insurance Effectively

Decline the Rental Company's Coverage: If you're using your credit card's rental car insurance, make sure to decline any additional coverage offered by the rental agency to avoid unnecessary costs.

Understand Coverage Limits: Be aware of your credit card's specific coverage limits and any exclusions that might apply, like specific vehicle types (luxury cars, trucks, etc.).

Documentation: Keep thorough documentation, including the rental agreement, receipts, and any accident reports in case you need to file a claim for damages.

5. Travel Insurance

a. Coverage Types

Many premium credit cards offer travel insurance as a built-in benefit, which can include trip cancellation insurance, travel accident insurance, and emergency medical coverage.

b. Leveraging Travel Insurance Benefits

Read the Policy: Familiarize yourself with what type of coverage is provided, as well as the claim limits. This knowledge will be helpful if you need to utilize your benefits in the event of a travel mishap.

Use Your Card for Booking: Most travel insurance benefits require that you pay for your tickets or accommodations with the card to activate the related coverage.

Maintain Records: Keep copies of itineraries, tickets, receipts, and any communication with airlines or hotels—all of which may be required when filing a claim.

6. Concierge Services

a. What are Concierge Services? Activated primarily through premium credit cards, concierge services provide cardholders with assistance on a wide range of requests, from making dinner reservations to arranging travel itineraries or even accessing exclusive events.

b. Making the Most of Concierge Services

Communicate Your Needs: Use the concierge service for ideas related to planning travel, sourcing luxury experiences, or obtaining hard-to-get reservations. The more accurate your requests, the better service you'll get in fulfilling them.

Compare Services: Not all concierge services operate the same, so it may be beneficial to test different request types to see which card's concierge provides the best options aligned with your preferences.

Use Their Expertise: Often, concierges have relationships with providers that lead to exclusive benefits like upgraded accommodations or discounts. Don't hesitate to ask them for recommendations or special arrangements.

7. Accessing Airport Lounge Benefits: Many premium credit cards provide access to airport lounge networks, allowing cardholders to escape the stresses of busy terminals while enjoying complimentary refreshments and comfortable seating.

a. Using Lounge Passes

Stay Updated on Lounges: Research which lounges you can access with your card. Some cards provide access to networks like Priority Pass, while others feature their own affiliated lounges.

Travel Benefits: Consider scheduling your travel times to allow for early arrivals at airports so you can take advantage of lounge access before flights.

Invite Guests: Many cards grant guest privileges, so be aware of guest policies to enhance travel experiences for family and friends.

Maximizing Your Cardholder Experience

8. Keep a Benefit Checklist: Create a checklist to understand and remember the benefits associated with each of your credit cards. This living
document can help you track when and how to utilize benefits effectively.

9. Stay Informed About Changes: Credit card terms, rewards structures, and benefits can change. Regularly review communications from your credit card issuer and revisit your cardholder agreements periodically to ensure you are getting the most updated information on your account.

10. Evaluate and Adjust: As you become more aware of the cardholder benefits you use most frequently, periodically evaluate your credit card portfolio. You may choose to switch to different cards that offer more aligned benefits or even additional perks that would benefit your lifestyle and current needs.

Incorporating cardholder benefits beyond rewards into your financial strategy can significantly amplify the overall value you receive from your credit cards. By effectively leveraging purchase protection, extended warranties, price matching, rental car insurance, travel insurance, concierge services, and airport lounge access, you can enjoy a richer experience, protect your purchases, and save money in the long run.

As you continue your journey through the world of credit cards, remember that staying informed and proactive is key. By understanding and utilizing the array of benefits available, you not only optimize your spending and redeeming strategies but also enhance your quality of life—making the most of every dollar spent and every benefit offered.

The journey toward financial empowerment and savvy spending doesn't end here; it's just the beginning.

$$$$$$$$$

Chapter 20

Final Tips on Staying Organized and Tracking Rewards

As you journey through the intricate landscape of credit card rewards, organization and tracking become essential skills that can dramatically impact your financial efficiency and satisfaction. With an ever-increasing array of credit cards, reward programs, and associated benefits, it is crucial to maintain a clear overview of your rewards balances, redemption options, and expiration dates.

In this chapter, we will discuss best practices for tracking rewards and keeping an eye on expiration dates, as well as exploring tools and apps designed to help you manage multiple cards and reward points effectively.

Best Practices for Tracking Rewards and Expiration Dates

1. Know Your Rewards Programs: Before diving into tracking strategies, it is vital to have an understanding of the various rewards programs associated with each of your credit cards. Each program may have different earning structures, points valuation, redemption options, and expiration policies.

a. Create a Reward Summary Sheet: Design a spreadsheet to summarize each of your rewards programs, including: Card issuer, Type of rewards (cash back, travel points, etc.), Points balance, Expiration dates, Minimum redemption amounts and options. This document will serve as a centralized hub for all critical information related to your rewards, making it easier to track and manage.

2. Monitor Expiration Dates: Knowing when your rewards or points expire is crucial to maximizing their value. Many rewards programs implement strict expiration policies, which can catch users off-guard.

a. Set Reminders: Use digital calendars or task management apps to log expiration dates for each of your rewards programs.

Set reminders a few months in advance to give yourself ample time to find opportunities to utilize expiring points. This habit will help you avoid losing valuable rewards.

b. Check Programs Regularly: Regularly log into your rewards accounts (at least once every couple of months) to check your point balances and expiration dates.

Pay special attention to any communications from credit card issuers about changes, promotions, or impending expirations.

3. Redemption Strategy: Have a clear strategy when it comes to redeeming points. Consider a set timeline for when you'll redeem points, whether monthly, quarterly, or annually, based on your spending habits and travel plans.

a. Establish a "Use It or Lose It" Policy: Determine which cards or rewards programs require more immediate attention based on expiring points. Combine redemption strategies to maximize value; plan vacations or purchases to coincide with expiring rewards to prevent pointless loss.

b. Prioritize High-Value Redemptions: Focus on redeeming points that offer the highest value for travel purposes before considering low-value alternatives like gift cards or cash back.

4. Recording Points Earned and Spent: As you earn and redeem rewards, maintain a record of both to better understand your spending patterns and how effectively you're utilizing your points.

a. Maintain a Rewards Log: Create a log to keep track of points earned and spent, with dates and categories. For instance, separate travel, dining, and shopping categories. This practice will help you analyze which areas yield the best rewards.

Document any promotional offers or bonuses as they come up, ensuring that you can reproduce those strategies in the future for even greater benefit.

Tools and Apps for Managing Multiple Cards and Reward Points: As you accumulate multiple credit cards and diverse reward programs, managing them can become challenging. Fortunately, various tools and apps can streamline this process.

1. Reward Points Tracking Apps

a. AwardWallet Overview: AwardWallet is a popular tool that allows you to track various loyalty programs, including airline miles, hotel points, and credit card rewards.

Features: Automatically updates point balances. Sends alerts for expiration dates. Organizes all your reward accounts in one place.

b. Points.com Overview: Points.com provides a platform to manage various loyalty programs and allows you to exchange points between programs.

Features: Track point balances across multiple accounts. Offers options for buying, converting, or redeeming points.

c. Travel Freely Overview: Travel Freely is aimed at travel enthusiasts, helping you track your credit cards and maximize rewards.

Features: Users can input and track different credit card categories. Suggestions for optimized credit card usage based on spending habits.

2. Expense Tracking Apps: In addition to reward tracking, expense tracking apps can help you see how your spending aligns with your rewards strategy.

a. Mint Overview: Mint is a comprehensive budgeting tool that helps you track your spending across multiple accounts and budget your finances.

Features: Connect all financial accounts, including credit cards. Provides insights into your spending patterns and potential to optimize reward earning opportunities.

b. YNAB (You Need a Budget) Overview: A robust budgeting app that helps you allocate funds wisely and track expenses effectively.

Features: Emphasizes proactive budgeting, encouraging users to strategize their future expenses and credit card usage.

3. Reminder Apps: Setting reminders for key dates related to rewards is vital. Here are a couple of options:

a. Todoist Overview: A flexible task manager that allows you to set reminders for various tasks, including tracking expiration dates.

Features: Create projects for each credit card rewards program. Set recurring reminders to check rewards balances and schedule redemption efforts.

b. Google Calendar Overview: You can use this to set reminders for numerous dates and appointments, including expiration.

Features: Create monthly calendar events to check points, and add notifications for the desired timeline.

4. Credit Card Management Apps: With numerous credit cards comes the challenge of managing them effectively.

a. Credit Karma Overview: A financial management app that provides insights about credit scores and monitoring.

Features: Allows users to manage multiple credit cards from one platform. Provides updates and alerts tailored to the credit card usage and performance.

b. CardPointers Overview: CardPointers is tailored to educate users on how to optimize spending across multiple cards efficiently.

Features: Notify which card to use based on reward rates for specific categories. Track and compare various rewards programs.

Staying organized and effectively tracking your rewards and benefits are crucial components of optimizing the value you get from your credit cards.

By implementing the best practices discussed in this chapter—such as using a rewards summary sheet, monitoring expiration dates, maintaining a rewards log, and employing various tools and apps to streamline management, you'll be better equipped to make informed financial decisions.

Mastering the art of rewards organization will enhance your confidence in navigating the credit card rewards landscape, allowing you to earn the rewards you deserve while ensuring you maximize their value before they expire.

The world of credit cards can be complex, but with the right tools and strategies at your disposal, you can confidently manage your rewards and achieve your financial goals.

END